POEMS BY PADRAIC FALLON

PADRAIC FALLON

POEMS

THE DOLMEN PRESS

Set in Baskerville type
and printed and published at the Dolmen Press,
North Richmond Industrial Estate, North Richmond Street,
Dublin 1, Ireland
ISBN 0 85105 2355 THE DOLMEN PRESS

First Edition, 1974

Distributed in Ireland by
The Educational Company of Ireland Limited,
Walkinstown, Dublin 12

Distributed outside Ireland by Oxford University Press
except in the U.S.A. and in Canada
Distributed in the U.S.A. and in Canada by
Humanities Press Inc.
171 First Avenue, Atlantic Highlands, N.J. 07716

© *Padraic Fallon, 1974*

CONTENTS

ACKNOWLEDGEMENT

Acknowledgement is made to An Chomhairle Ealaíon (The Arts Council of Ireland) for their assistance in the production of this book.

I

AN ISLAND

A man must go naked to an island,
Let the weather lend
A skin till he grows one, the rock fit
The beat of the surftop to
His feet; let him go like spindrift
Till he find wings, or the wave
Streamline him like the great
Matter of a seal.

Let him find toes too,
Prehensile or web, for the cliff fall;
Let him put two notes in his pipe
And be the first music.
Let the island be the eye
And the boundary of his being, then
Let him be an island
And bound on his own beat,

Back before Gods,
Before the beginning, before the betrayal,
Before the woman slopped over on his bed
Before the sun stood on a stone circle;
Let him go back to be
Just one simple thing, matter, an island
At its first meeting with the sea.

COASTAL WATERS

HOLY WELL

In the annals saints
Sit in holy wells, talk freely
To grim hermits, heal
Who ails, the foot-holy
Pilgrims who walk in wishes.

The dumb speak, the cripple
Walks, the blind
Find the dazzling world of the mind
In new pigments. Here
The ways of God seem wayward but very dear.

Speak the word, Saint,
In your welling mineral
That world in a bright and single jet
Go up, and inside it, lit up,
God my space and my material.

THE DWELLING

At night the house grows
Around the blackshawled woman. Harsh
And sparse the bony room
But with the lamp
All the pieces give their lights:
She shines among her satellites.

Man-chairs of oak, scrubbed; a rack
Of cups and blue plates;
The tabled jug:
The oilcloth spreading from the wick;
The spindled stair without a rug
But scrubbed, scrubbed to the quick.

The tiny window's shut its eye;
Let the strand roar
And the white horses tumble on the shore,
Here catgreen
The salt driftwood purrs inside the fire
And the sea ends that pours around the world.

Somewhere an old working clock,
Weights and chains, ticks on and tells
The woman's hours;
The wether's wool in the knitted sock,
The world weather in
Her knotted face, her knotted talk;

How men come home
From the ocean drip, still rocking, ill at ease
Till she gathers them;
Here she sets them down in peace
Inside the lamp, the house, the shawl.
Here is the centre of them all.

And all the pieces hang
In one. The man is on the chair
Who winds the clock
Who'll climb the stairhead after her,
Adjust the wick
Till the great night idles, barely ticking over.

Old men bleed
Quietly into one another, the gossips
Of summer and seaweed
Unhinged now from giant epics

And with as little space as
Dead starfish, they who
Sank with the mercury down
The Pole and broke holes in the blue

And rode their timbers out through a welter
Of geography, die slowly.
What they made was rich
But has no history

And leaves nothing, no body
That might reverberate
Like the small whorled compass of a shell
That stacked away a world of light;

Hobbling aboard the stone jetty,
Crutched and woolled, they cackle to their peers;
Conches they need, sea-trumpets
To bring back the bellowing years,

Not this uncertain pianissimo
To winter arteries and the dead leaves
Of their shredded hands;
Their number less by tomorrow. And who grieves

Outside the ever dwindling circle?
Who'll understand
Their mountains of water, or their daily
Victories far off land.

CAPRICORNIAN

In a quiet place,
Sea-locked, the moon is the pendulum
And the year the only face
Scanned for time;
The figures turn through the sun;
Twelve ancients stand on the horizon.

Nearer then the twelve
Gazeboes in their old star houses
Is the ram that rounds his horn on the hill;
The stone donkey by the wall
Is humble, has no wings; Taurus
Never stamped a cow like my black bull;

And my mother goat steps daintily
From ledge to ledge, ignores the fabulous
Ocean; she
Too is no heraldry, offers us
A full udder to fill the cans and
Occasionally brings forth twins

The old people love
To dine on, like
That old poet with his Falernian. He, too,
Found spring wells holy, some
God hung above
The natural bubble, his bright kingdom come;

Feared the sea god
Who locks havens, the sky piled
With wilder fellows, the uncontrollable;
Yet on a May day from the gorse
The eye sees fairly
A peopled sea, the hulls in a haze of morse;

And from our wedge
Of world, here on the very edge
Feel the one and the various move upon the spindle,
But the god singular,
An islandman
Who touches the chimney pots with smoke, who is a
    calendar

Of everyday affairs, a neighbour's voice,
A woman at the churn,
A child in wonder at the half door,
The split pollock drying in the sun,
The boats pulled up and
All night the moon, the pendulum.

DAY ASHORE

Sundays the long boat of the week
Is drawn up, turned keel over on the sand;
Rest, fellows, on the old
Wall, bellying the wind.

Here the sea colour shoals
And the Pole fails to pull. Rest, fellows,
On your rock pillows
And the small seas that sleep in shells.

Tomorrow the heave as earth turns over
Into Monday. Take your ease.
Light the pipe. Sit on forever.
Forget you're cold saltwater to the knees.

Oro, the islandmen
Load herring from the white shoals
Into the barrows of the shawled fishwives
On the grey wall of Galway:
And lightly where sunlight was warehoused by the water
From the tarred hulls they sway
In their blue homespuns and skin shoes
To the hazy wall and away.

O tell me what lazy Peeler
Thumbing his girth will dare them
Now money that ripens like rain on ropes
Runs down their hasty fingers?
And what fat terrified son of the devil
That tends a till won't pull back porter
All night for men whose eyes make knives
Of the lights that worm through his bottled windows?

But quietly at last as a sheep-fair
From the old square the day disperses,
One spark of the sun stands hitched
Like a lonely ram in a corner,
And Padraic the son of Patcheen Rua
Shakes the drink from the wild top of his skull
And stoops from the door in his whispering shoes
To dandle the sky on his shoulder.

O grey city
Of stone and mist and water,
Here's terror, a son of Clan Flaherty
Footloose in your sleepy air.

Have you no shocked sudden memory
Of rape and ringing steeple
As he grows in a lane, towering, till the sea
Seems no more size than a mackerel?

Fly for the bishop, quick.
Call all the lazy constables for, O,
By Padraic Patcheen Rua now
An innocent woman idles.
Bright in the midnight of her shawl
Her face rises, in her own light
Her piled hair slipping from the comb
Could hide a lover out of sight.

O, Padraic Patcheen Rua, such a woman
Never had a match
In any thatched house on the windy island;
And, O, Padraic, did she stretch
On the top of a headland with you of an evening
What riches your great hand would win
Burning on all her slow horizons down
From crown to shin.

Man, dear, do you dawdle
And the world before you?
A ship with two sails
And a gallow's crew,
And the wind right for Connemara
Where you will have your will
And potheen in a jug
By a three-legged stool?

Open your mouth, O dolt.
Strike the great silver string.
Give the gossips a story, we sicken
Of talking of tides and fish.
Lay hands on her, show her the rocks
And rainbows of water we twist
Out of ourselves for the women, taking
An ocean on the bowsprit.

Are you making a mock of us, Padraic?
Is an islandman backing
Round like a colt if a woman
But finger his elbow?
By God, do you turn and run
And she trying to hold you
So hard that you leave in her two hands
Three parts of your woollen waistcoat?

O, your wife will magnify you
To our wives at the chapel door.
And a hundred and twenty-seven saints whose bones
Are green grass in Killeaney
Will praise you with praises flashing on the eaves
Of heaven like wintry drops of rain.
But what of us, Padraic, what of us,
Men raised to the sea?

GOWRAN PARK, AUTUMN MEETING

The year's potatoes, they've ploughed them out,
The threshing rig's gone round about;
Earth finishes with the harvest time.

A low sun noses through the damps;
The trees are bare down to the stumps;
A mist can spring up white as lime.

The fox is red as the huntsman's coat,
The doublebarrel rhymes a note,
The season turns on the hill;

But day sits up like a hunkered hare
As horse and jockey catch the roar;
Gowran lights like a paper spill.

Soon long shadows will creep from the grill
Of every gate, the mountains stamp,
The year fall into the Christmas lamp.

CURRAGH, NOVEMBER MEETING

Distances are
Threaded over, a web. And the same spider
Spins the tale of
The dying sun

Caught on his last legs. Bleaching too
Are the bright horses: Jackets
And jockeys run
Out of pigment, are

A caveman's scratches, a jostling script.
There's some time left
To use your magic on it, wish
The winner home

Down Walsh's hill into
The drumbeat of the straight. Here
We go offering
The thing a heart, the spectacle a home:

And half ashamed of it, the child's
Play, the toys in colour now
Thumping their own life out of us, galloping
Into the heart

And away. Gone. Tomorrow the
Empty stands, the moneyspinner in
His winter coat;
And all forgotten.
                    Nomads no more

It means nothing, nor should; a mock-up
Since we dropped that wild pulse settling down at last,
Suburban fathers: or at most a slight
Affair with a trumpet blast.

TRADESMEN'S ENTRANCE

LOVE

I

The strong man
Is he only after all the creature of what seems
Desirable, whom nothing else can
Please because once it was all the boy's dreams?

A girl on a horse
In the leaves of autumn, in the careless havoc of the air;
Behind her over the lawn the big house,
And she the prouder for that house there.

Magnificent the dream
To the boy who peers from the wall. She gallops on
But never away, the house there all the time,
Skies unmoving, the journey never done.

II

Ring out
Bells, give the lads a holiday;
Shutters down and shops shut, a stout
In every fist. It's love will find a way.

Love, or its dunce
The desperation that throws in its hand
Before the miracle happens that for the nonce
Will open up the land.

Is it always she,
The first, the almost forgotten, some ancient lie
That shattered us with truth, who is the enemy
And must be triumphed over for the boy?

Bless them. Ring, Bells.
They are what they are, they have what they have, enough
For whom the bell tolls
To tell their desperate stuff.

PEASANTRY

In a thatch
That could be a stable but for the open hearth
A man is born, the tiller of the earth.
Labour there, dumb brothers,
And have no wild itch
To raise yourselves. The world is to your betters.

In the Mall,
Discreetly behind curtains, servants wait
On money that makes itself early and late;
And with the cash goes credit
And breeding, all
Ripening of the person. This the rich inherit.

Walk the town,
Tiller, interloper, up and down, we
Who live upon you will allow this free,
But close our heavy doors
To any clown
Born to the thatch in the boor-stink of the byres.

The lodestoned salmon, hurtling
Always in the right direction, find
The trickle of their birth,
Stand fantailed on the falls
And somersault into the milting weather.

Whole gravels are in rut.
The ocean has come home to melt away
The salt, to lie under
A maybush and almost tenderly
Suck from the lazy heavens a blue-green fly.

On love's seething house,
Rocking the thousand cradles, the first fresh
Will fall and the spent bulls
Drop with it down the slow river spirals;
Aching for space now the once rampant males;

Caught here in their bored
Congregations, while the wandering nerve
Twitches towards Norway. How many years
Since I first saw the stones waver,
The river paving turn to fins and tails?

Loafing a lunch hour in the sun,
And here's the wheel come round again;
So much to do, so little done;
The tiny trickle of my birth
Dwindling back into the earth.

VOWELS

A: Watermaid, the frantic virgin who
Yet hides her birth where man must hatch it, E:
Distant and elongated drapery,
The lady-never-won whom all men woo,
O: midsummer woman, countryside
And sway, the opulent bed, the wed, the bride.
U: is my mother gathering up the view,
Majestic, with an apple on her knee.

But I: I, is my danger; my knotted thread
And needle's eye; my ancient grandmother
Who tells my follies while she sews my shroud.
At times she fades as if not made of matter,
And then again her glance is all a glitter
When she lifts her shears and chatters with the dead.

FIN DE SIECLE

He'd seen them off, some down
The gutters of the stews,
Scarcely awake, sad drunks
And disastrous lovers as they say;
He'd seen the manias take over;
And even Wilde, for all
His heraldry, die maudlin:

Never his hailfellows exactly;
Golden boys to whom
The Muses hearkened at the well already,
And the rampant horse came
At the first call;
They were the early promisers
High upon the swaying feathers

At a time when he
Was kicking along the old gelded spavin,
Mild as a monk, they were high up there
Engaging the whole heaven;
Icarus had a like fall, melting
Down before anything big could happen;
But those were the Muse driven

Who'd seen the shocking vision and lived on;
Those were the harassed
And the lost;
In the wide world no comforter:
Into the earth's dumb side
The big horse stamped them, waiting
For the next victim, the next master,

Who was you-know-who,
The unlikeliest, like the lucky youngest brother
Whose faery godmother said: 'Go slow!
Take it easy;
Disaster
Is the portion of the young. Who lives long
Enough will make a master.'

Out on the periphery he put in the time;
Achilles dead, and Hector, Ulysses flown
And he the brighter for the falling bolts.
Who makes the rhyme
Will have the resonance. Carefully
He lived to tell the tale;
Homer is he who survives the crumbling wall.

He shakes a carefully shaggy head;
Oddly he is not comforted;
The years round on him;
The unspent shekels jangle in
The too-careful flesh. Oh the abandon
They had, who were all mad youth,
Suicide and singing mouth.

They troop by, uncalled. The wanton
Stares are bright; Shades are reasserting
The sole right of Youth, which is
Merely to be beautiful.
The mockery.
This old body wandering on his wall,
Mock tower, mock battlements,
And out there all the glory of the fall;

And the abyss, the horse
No longer mild and nickering. Try the ride,
Old body, be
The most famous suicide.
A bit unsound in wind, heavy of limb,
He rises from his years, to find
A great carnivorous creature under him.

MA BOHEME
after Rimbaud

So I tramped the roads, my hands through my torn
    pockets,
My old coat just a ghost about to vanish;
I was your tramp, Muse, but rich, with worlds to lavish,
La, la, the marvels we dream of, we mad poets!

I rhymed with my buttocks falling out like moons
Through holes in my trousers, uncaring, my head in the
    air;
I took a room each night in the Great Bear;
Stars over my distant hair had the soft swish of gowns.

And I listened, excited with dew as with strong wine,
At my ease in a ditch, a mood, a creature of starshine
In the good September twilights, a man apart,

And rhyming, rhyming, while all the darks took root,
I tucked one leg like a lyre about my heart
And strummed the elastic of my broken boot.

J' ACCUSE

These are curls on his head,
Not rings of mail, General. They will not save him
From gun-butt or bayonet.
They please the eye and maybe someone's fingers.

That eager and innocent look
That meets you, General, is not armour-plated,
Not built, indeed, for the bullet
Issued today, you remember signing form this-and-that?

This perfect and gambolling body,
A marvel, General, eh? And well it might be,
Begotten as it was in love.
Alas, there is no bomb-shelter it can carry.

No place for my son safe,
No new planet, General, for you too would be there
To guard us early and late
From every possible and impossible invader.

And yet he will be killed, he is already dead,
General, of I know not what missile or poison. And his
    mother
Will not speak to me. Not a word is said
Between us two who were lover and lover.

Why does she accuse me,
General, with such white and disfigured silence? You
Will know surely, you can tell me.
You know such a lot you can tell me surely.

Is it because you had a father
Who didn't, General, strangle you at birth,
Or after, when you started playing soldier
On the table, before that table became the earth?

POETE MAUDIT

Mad as metaphor
You, Rimbaud, once. O petit amasseur des rentes,
When you buried the god did all the marvellous rant
Stop, or still seek in you the saviour?

You who were language to a field,
And a wood's identity walking, who felt silence
Turn its stones into birds when you were the all once
And worlds in words of glass revealed

Was there other sanity
After all that? Was he sane, the dead-eyed man
With the vision of a levelled gun
And all the inanity?

Adding all that never shows
Into a tradesman's ledger, the weeping nail-holes
In his hands, the unfeathered heels,
That forehead where a crown of thorns grows:

You who opened like a rose
Inside the very heart of contemplation
Where the poet oozes blood that's not his own,
You, the flower and the cross,

The harmony of agony
And agony of harmony beyond thought;
Poet, when you buried the god, did Nothing still seek
    you out
In the night like sweat, a dark anxiety,

And maunder on and on
In its no-language, fumbling for the ghost
And the wild metaphor of the lost
And living god you buried under stone?

THE CAT
after 'La Géante' by Baudelaire

My time was then, before Earth tamed volcanoes
To fold their petals quietly as a rose,
When from her loves Nature had who knows
What strange children in mighty ebbs and flows.

I could have been a cat, voluptuously
Curious on the knees of a huge young queen
While she flowered in large sweet tremors under me,
Wooed but wondering, lost, and longingly obscene.

To trouble her look with a male and secret stare,
Green as glass, and then, O love, to wander
The great valleys of her loosening knees

Or sometimes in summer evenings when she rests
Stretched out like a countryside, to take my ease
Like a sleepy mountain village on her breasts.

II

A FLASK OF BRANDY

You, said the Lionwoman,
Pliz, this errand, a snipe of brandy
From the first shop. Here's money;
And for you this penny.

And on my way I saw:
Item, a clown who waltzed on stilts;
A bear saluting with a paw;
Two pairs of dancing dogs in kilts;
Eight midget ponies in a single file,
A very piccolo of ponies;
Then the princess far off in her smile;
And the seven beautiful distant ladies:
And then —

Facing after the big bandwaggon, he
The boy in spangles, lonely and profound:
Behind him the Ringmaster, a redfaced man,
Followed by silence heavy as a wound,
And empty.

Quickly as two feet can did I come back
To the Lionwoman with her cognac.

You, said the Lionwoman;
Pliz to the window, said foreign gutterals in
The cave of the caravan.
I waited, errand done.

And waiting on one foot saw:
Item, a twitching coloured chintz
Moved by a lemontaloned claw:
And after a woman with her face in paints,
A throat thickened in its round of tan
On shoulders sick and white with nature;
Behind was a pair of bloomers on a line,
Blue; A table with a tin platter:
More else:

A black electric cat, a stove, a pot
Purring, and a wild Red Indian blanket
Crouching sidewise on a bunk;
And some exciting smell that stunk
Till the Lionwoman rising blotted out
All but a breast as heavy as a sigh
That stared at me from one bruised eye.

THE YOUNG FENIANS

They looked so good;
They were the coloured lithographs
Of Murat, Bernadotte and Ney
And the little Corsican.
Mars had made them from our dead
And given to each his martial head.

The cavalry and plumes would come,
No doubt about it;
Every half-acre man with a sword,
The boy with a drum;
And down the Alps of every local hill
The bannered horses ride to kill.

O'Connell helpless in the house;
The old gazeboes at their talk,
All to no purpose;
Tone must rise and Emmet walk,
Edward troop out of Kildare;
The time had come; the day was fair.

Flags flew from our every word;
The new names sang from litanies,
Saviours each one;
They were the eagles in the morning sun;
A country rising from its knees
To upset all the histories.

WEXFORD TO COMMODORE BARRY

When the story
Reaches the stage of bronze, the omens
That sang are dead too; the glory
All that remains.
It is little enough
Even when man still wears his earthly stuff.

Good Hero and
All American man, that other lord
Of spear and trumpet, Achilles, banned
And blue in Hades, put it in a word;
Death is the worst thing:
Life makes every petty drudge a king.

Do not, for God's sake,
Envy old schoonermen, your mates
On the water who can still kick:
Life too satiates,
And they have only breath
Enough to admire you for your lack of death.

In the Bally of your birth
They say no braveries were allowed;
Small houses laboured up from bits of earth,
And lest soul turn to mud,
Man thatched the things; and so, to put it raw,
Friend, Bronzefellow, you were a man of straw

With your back bent
Early. To lords and hunger you
Bowed uneasily, paying the usual rent,

Not yet thinking how
Far out beyond bondage a boy could go
Over oceans of himself to make his harbour stow.

The boy made man;
The boy who'd but a beggar's rights to the road
Threw all his thread on the open ocean
And found how threatening latitudes
Expand. Now, tall as ships can be,
On the earth's round ripple you stand up at sea.

So, Bronzefellow, we
On this waterledge find you comfort us;
Success of a kind is poetry,
A headline we miss.
'Aye', sigh some, 'our John brought home the gravy.'
But you made from the Irish chip an oaken Navy.

JOHNSTOWN CASTLE

I

The summer woods refuse to meet
Us on the levels we know. We have evolved
Too much mind for them, and picked up feet
That solve things differently, like birds:
Trees use the old vocabulary
In all its ponderous gravity;
We with inner needs to be resolved
Have learned all the new and air-borne words.

Why intrude here, and why regret
An old root that like a rocket goes
On exploding season after season
In the same galaxy of leaf, without a reason?
All it knows
Is the old wholesome suit of clothes:
Never the new and complicated rose.

II

An ornamental water
Should be backed with mercury that the sculptured swan
May be ideal swan forever.
Here one shiver shows the mud
And I am glad because a swan
Can turn up his end and shatter mood
And shatter mirror,
Till the woods massed in an architecture shake
Because a real swan mucks up a lake.

An old lady, slender as her wand
Of ebony, and carrying her castle still about her,
Is near me anywhere I stand;
My own creation.
I give her words to say, and a world, too,
Homelier, perhaps, than that she knew,
And take an interest in the conversation:
But as I ramble on
Creating all for her
I think how certainly she lived this view
Merely by walking over the ground
Day after day; I falter
For now my words take on another hue
And such a sound
I'm half afraid to turn around.

III

Always my own monologue
Intrudes; things work into the word
Only to be imprisoned, or kennelled like a dog;
So the tall pine describes
A straight line up to the tuft of foliage
That sits it like a bird
And is only so much language
Because I use the word;
And all the ponderous oaks and the ooze underfoot,
All the harsh nerves of an old wood
That are a rumble in the nether-gut,
Are not what one transcribes
And never any good;
The monologue intrudes, my words let me
Into a poem, not into the poetry.

And yet a man must walk
Out of his mystery, if he's to meet it
Face to face, in talk,
And guess from words omitted the major and delicate
Evasions of his ghost
Who is the host
To every massive feeling and must live it.
Create me, says the poet, I am a body
For every word, the large word that was lost
And the word you'd throw a dog;
Transform me who travel towards infinity
In a makeshift monologue.

BOYNE VALLEY

On a mound chipped
From the dead, deity
And scantlings dismantled, the spell broken,
I stand on a stone ship
That sails nowhere

But once was set right to launch
The bronze and brandished hero, fellow
Of this same sun that low now
In bare twigs
Lies lumped in the winter's wicker basket,

Who was laid in
This hill of metaphor, as if a grave has no end,
Suspended in some state of grace above
His own diving depths,
To find North like the barnacle

And a quite definite eternal Paradise
(Only the best admitted, Stags
Of the year, Gods
In the demi-brackets) not very different from this;
But Paradise is always somewhere else,

Leaving his head to the stone axe, and the big, broken
Torque of his body to dangle,
Wail, ye women,
God is dead
And picked over by this year's summer students,

Whose secret name was
A flight of months, the whole earth offering
Its barbarous alphabet to make him delicate;
Now trees and stones have forgotten; the birds
Are entirely without auspices

And preen flit strut in winter attitudes,
Birds, not litanies. The thing is gone
Now that no giant drops from the gaudy zenith
Like Mad Sweeney
To hang on the last Elder tree head and antlers.

Flayed, to be scattered in this the thirteenth
Unlucky month, for Fertility, for a patch
Of emmer barley, for all men —
To give their guts literally to this, —
To Demeter the first plough.

A sow, snouted with the moon's horn! But
It's Isis I think of, Magna Mater, to whom
The divine members from their schism clambered;
Into the magnet they came, the brilliant head
Topping the whole winged tread again —

Meaning just a new sun
On the old wheel, the one wheel, and world safe inside
The big roll of gravity, but
Aware there is a moment
When all things could fall in,

As indeed they may,
For all this peaceful scene, Boyne cease to flow
Broad through this green valley with
Its copious flood
Of ephemeral nature notes,

Such as one swaying sunheaded reed,
Such as a crow daubed on the ripple of
A black poplar, a thrusting ash
In its hedgeleap carrying
The long horizon on a twig, twice.

Distantly a horn, not Herne and his hounds but
Esquires at play, a near hill rolls gold
For some unearthly reason,
And maybe too this battered helmet of a place
I straddle cold

With sheep suddenly on the fosse;
Souls? No, merely ewes
And wearing the ram's pigments, the autumn's raddle;
Fertility minds its own business;
And world will go on more or less

The same notwithstanding God
Or Goddess; only man the danger. Still
It must be heartening in ill times to have
Ties with the whole network,
God on the wire inside a hill.

Jaguars roll from the meet, trailing
Horseheads and dogfoxes. History
Is slowly reaching some conclusion somewhere:
And here is the usual tentative dusk
As day runs out of silver

And one flintnebbed swan owns all the Boyne;
No afterglow or
Gold bowl to sail home the antlered one,
Surrogate, heraldic sufferer,
Cerumnos, Arthur, Bran.

THE HEAD

I

The day after decapitation
Was no wound yet. Noon found the head
Excited still and still singing
The visionary woman, still exalting
The woman in measures to which no words came
Off the black tongue. The river flies
Were busy on specks of blood, in clouds upon the hair;
But where her praise was fixed upon his face
No one had died, the flesh was adequate;
And on a mouth that seemed alive
Only the smile was anti-clockwise;
But no wound yet.

That night it drifted on
Through stars that buzzed no brighter, inches
Of radiance before it and around
That felt no wound;
And this was dyed with a flutter of vague moths,
And overhead where a curious white owl
Dilated, there was some reflection too;
And down below
More of it and stranger for the eels
Had scented blood and wavered under the wicker;
This was a head that trickled down many tails
Into the deeps, eddying without end;
And still was felt no wound.

The slow morning came
Back to the eyes and brought the labouring crow
(Corvus corax corax) who discharged himself
Upon the skull unskilfully and cawed
Once, twice, and there for long was still.

45

The gulls disturbed him when the eyes were gone
And over the bloody mess rose such confusion
Three salmon fishers rowed out from a draft
Only to retch their morning stirabout:
That noon the skull gaped
And still was felt no wound.

The second afternoon it rained;

Rinsing the ruin the nozzled drops removed
Sundry strips, tissues, barber's clippings,
Odds of nerves, bits, leaving such scrags, jags
And rags as still clung and dripped
To shine strangely when the sun came out.
The waters steamed a little before night
And from the skull where little pools remained
There oozed a smoke, a vagrant and hairlike smoke;
And in the hollow eyes the rain
Was bright as sight, and so it seemed
The nose put forth its bridge again,
And from the earholes arched two tufts of fawn,
Two gilded wisps, the ears. The face had dreamed
Itself right back again.
And still no pain;
Still the exultant thing was fixed, and dawn
Found the bare teeth beautiful.

II
The third day repeated as before
Washed out the skullhouse and refurnished it
With the changeable midsummer weather:
The head alone at last
Was bonebare and beaming; and where it floated
Down the broad vowel of the river, once
Its song was heard;

46

Snatches only, faint upon the ripple
And weirs of the water-word: A thin
Piping.

The reeds heavytopped tipped to it
As to a breeze.

         So it was the wind
That used the tattered wizen of the throat
As well as the sockets of the eyes, the earholes
And the pit behind the nose for hollow music,
Not overlooking the jewels of the mouth
That still smiled
For yet no wound was felt.

So time stopped
Outwardly, but there was still this woman
In the weather of the head
Who was all time to it no longer human.
And in that time the head came

By stages of water world
From green granaries, tilled, from fat uddered
Cow-lawns by river houses, woods that spoke in oak
And heavy roots and clumped along the banks,
To a country narrow low and cold
And very thin like a wire,
Where the head sang all day.

There the seas fell inland almost vacantly
Over a sieve of sand;
There the head lay

While the coracle under it of sally withes
Dried, withered in sunlight, salt sealight,
Rotted till the ashen thwart that held the head
Rigid and singing, sprung the spent lashings,
Tipping over;
This, one day when the set from the southwest
Piled up an equinoctial on the coast;
On the white shore with no one to notice
The head fell.

And broke

In a separation of its major and distinct parts.
Two.

And from the still centre where was the true
Bubble or heartbeat, came the tiny whimper
Of some unhouselled thing;
The head's first cry
At last and never heard

By gull, gale, sandpiping bird
Or gannet in the tall and touselled blue,
Nor the wader on two pins nearby,
Though the cry was human,
The pain spreading greatly, going
Towards blood in every direction

But never arriving
Near and away where the woman was
Doing the usual things to men and clothes
Afraid of the glass,
Groundswell and undertows,
What happens and the happening
That will never come to pass.

48

A VISIT WEST

I

The town is an ideogram
Of a town with its square keep and the brush of smoke
From the baker's chimney,
Almost intact at first sight
With wall and moat and narrow gate.
The wooden horse is in the square.

Everywhere my uncle Ben
Emerges with a limp from a round tower;
And that's the poem I'd like to write,
The old boy tipping his rod to the wavy weather,
Fish hooks and feathers thrown
Over the windy edge of March;
He owns them all now, the streaming rivers
By inalienable right.

So humbly down the river lawn
I'd tail him with a tuppenny pole;
(Hare's Ear, March Brown)
Here was the soul who lived alone;
Gone before I'd reach the bridge
Far off on a desolate slab of sky
Tipped off the harsh Atlantic roof,
Fly size.

The wooden horse is in the square.
Urbs, they say, intacta, meaning
The virgin sleeps late;
Between yawns life goes on
With some cunning to
Accomplish itself.

49

Children are born,
To up and vanish like me,
Mostly;
There is no return, and the wound
There and leaching
Forever into the one and
Only summer;

Lost.
The wooden horse is in the square;
And Ben, old Ben.

II
To pay off the ghost, two
Bottles of brandy
Left with the nuns to dole out
Circumspectly;
White coif and wimple, heavenly
Barmaids.

What greater wrong could I have done
On this cantankerous spirit
Limping in from nowhere with nuts and trout
And wild apples
Who'd get most nobly drunk on a market day!

What now he's gone?
New slates and paintwashed shops,
A garage in a flower bed;
Hovel and seeding thatch swept from the lane
And the hag's head
Curing slowly on
The smoking half door, like ham.

III

He saw a lingering eighteenth century out,
The great mansions left
Embedded in the prosy land
Die of their heraldry;
Even saw the last rebellion start,
The wooden horse stand in the square.

And never gave the world a thought
As the vast familiar glacier melted down;
While Kaisers fell and navies sank he drowned
His pint glass in Glynn's,
Tallied his ewes abroad, his dog
Tucked at his heel, the West
Tumbling over him, his own sky
Strung from his fist.

Original
Inhabitant or feckless double
Opting out with his toy town and
Baby river,
An old primitive do-nothing who
Stabilised among the lesser shades
Can still pull

Me over the Shannon to lose me in
His greenery where the grass
Watches of the fields are stalled
Forever

And time is March and bright
Elysium
Where he disappears, his body gone
Into the weather
Without a care.

The wooden horse stands in the square.

YEATS AT ATHENRY PERHAPS

I

We had our towers too, a large
Stone soldiery at bridge and gateway, they
Were the whole town once;
And I could have nodded to him from the top
Tendril of ivy or a jackdaw's nest;
But I'd never heard of him, the famous poet,
Who lived as the crow flies fifteen miles away.

Certainly he'd have touched us changing trains
For Gort, have hours to idle, shared
The silence of our small town shell;
Maybe he passed me by
In a narrow gutted street, an aimless
Straying gentleman, and I
The jerseyed fellow driving out the cows.

Ours was a sightseeing place that had
Exhausted history, but old wars had left
A dead king and a moat
And walls still half alive that watched
From towers with broken rims. I doubt
He bothered with us, all his sight turned in;
Some poems come better waiting for a train.

And that winged footprint could have jarred
The peasant metres of a street given over
To baker, grocer, butcher and
The treadmill of the till. What would he think
Of our outcropping sheds, the architecture
Of the very necessary animal?
And little better our weathered famine chapel?

But on the Eve of May he might have found
Things near his heart, Fertilities
Dropping in;
For then from consecrated ground we moved
The Virgin to the leafing trees
With bonfires, chanting children, the whole works;
The Canon hadn't read the latest books
On golden boughs and odd divinities.

Or would he have looked superior, been difficult
About Our Lady's face, the soft Italian
Look of the milking mother, not the sort
That strings the whole air like a catapult?
This was no moon in women, no
Unpredictable lady sailing
Her wavy shell;
Ours kept the house and answered the chapel bell.

Or so we thought or didn't think at all.
Diana has her secrets from the oak;
The nunlike night commits itself in strokes
Of barbarous shorthand when the candles die.
What's fifteen miles? We could have read together
The same nightscript, felt the vibrations run,
Boughs singing, with the whole south moving up
To stand in a dripping arch of spring.

II

I'd like to think how over the sheep and crops,
The nut-creggs and the loose stone walls we met
In a mutual hazard of burning arrows, but
I was too small then, my wavelengths caught
In anything low-down as a hawthorn tree
And jammed there for a day or all the summer,
Time no object, profession poetry.

Anyway he wouldn't have dared a town
Where every peeling window was an eye;
We smiled of course at strangers, proud
Of a dead king, the lordly
Dung that simmered in the ground. But I could
Have walked him round the moat, in Kingsland shown
    the rock
Where the crown toppled from the last Irish head
And a royal footsole left a bloody track.

No, he'd have sat down by the line and waited
Melting his bits of ore or watched the sky
Jolt from the saltmills of the Atlantic over
A town that died so often of the rain;
Why muddy a feathered foot when a great house waited
Over in Coole among the trees
(He liked his heraldry alive, well baited)
With all the amenities for Muse and man,
Leda's kingbird on a lake, a lawn
For Juno's peacock, tranquil as a frieze.

KILTARTAN LEGEND

Penelope pulls home
Rogue-lord, artist, world wanderer,
Simply by sitting in a house,
Its sturdy genius;
Of all sirens the most dangerous.

She'll sit them out,
The curious wonders, the ventriloquial voices,
Spacious landfalls, the women, beds in the blue;
Her oceanography
The garden pond, her compass a knitting needle.

The arc-lamped earth, she knows,
Will burn away and she
Still potter among her flowers waiting for him;
Apollo runs before
Touching the blossoms, her unborn sons.

Knitting, unknitting at the half heard
Music of her tapestry, afraid
Of the sunburned body, the organs, the red beard
Of the unshipped mighty male
Home from the fairy tale;

Providing for him
All that's left of her she ties and knots
Threads everywhere; the luminous house
Must hold and will
Her trying warlord home.

Will she know him?
Dignity begs the question that must follow.
She bends to the web where her lord's face
Glitters but has no fellow,
And humbly, or most royally, adds her own.

ON THE TOWER STAIRS

I

Arrow slits with heads
Of bitter weather; even here on this
Stone spindle winding up I have to think of her,
A dugout deity, a disconcerting
Earth mother living on.

Outwardly just a plain
Dump of a woman; no planetary body this
To magnify or disintegrate, genius
To no man. Yet Symons
All crow and ominous had sensed the siren

That afternoon she'd dropped in at Tulyra
Where he and Yeats were summering. 'La Strega',
Quoth the Temple Beau sniffing
The quite ordinary meat —
Which makes no witch of her and no carnivorate

Nor a Beardsley black-and-white
Alive with insomnia in
Her widowed woods and swanlake. This was a lady
Given to no love
But a house and the glory thereof;

Stumping her walks for boundary and trespass;
And there was a diary
Voluminous, with the low trajectory
Of the Galway grass; and there was this
(Mr. Gregory's Postbag) biography

Of a long-gone dismal hack who'd dined
On the Castle periphery, another of the husband-father
Who from a simple
Bible household bare
As a tent translated her

To rooms where books
Were accepted inhabitants. He'd held the gorgeous
East in fee, somewhere a governor
Before her time —
Ceylon, I think, where the tea comes from

And elephants dance round Buddha's tooth.
Take it easy, this
Is a serious lady ready for a new
Dispensation. Did she know it
Watching him the gangling poet

In square, or is it trine, with Martyn's woods
Which rumour had it he was rocking
Some nights with lunar incantations?
What did she see
Beyond the too obvious anarchy,

Locust buzz and face of honey? The prophet authentic,
Like Midsummer John all lovely head?
Divining in
The endless budding of the wand
A lord of wine?

What were her chances?
A man with an arrow in his heart and a lifetime woman
More turbulent than a Muse;
And she with her cruise of oil half spent, in
The crepuscular shiver of the menopause?

II

A dumpy vernacular Victoria
Ruminating homewards to her moated bed,
(The very road I took this morning
In the downpour)
How did she manage it, capture the speaking head?

Maud Gonne from her hawklegged heights at eighty
    laughing
(Never in this tower she, never
On this stair)
'She did try to play Kathleen . . . but
She lisped so badly, poor dear'.

Vanity? (That bronze
In Charlemont House?) What does it matter now?
Who can question the work done?
I stand in the rainblitzed light
Outside, in the dogstare of the door.

Her trumpeted house is gone, entirely razed;
But he did raise up another
There on a totem pole in which the lady is
Oracular and quite composed
To outlast everything, live on forever.

STOP ON THE ROAD TO BALLYLEE

I read Horace here
Where the lunatics now shamble around
The wrong side of their shadows. Kore or the moon
Have no pity. Mouthfuls of air,
Said the Big Tower, that's what we are.

Q. Horatii Flacci Carminum Liber 1;
Elementary classics, small blue book, Macmillan.
Our soft Cs were true Italian.
                                    These
Overlay the place, shamblers
Stuck with the upper air,

Illustrating something, Limbo or something, not
Like Liber 1 with its fauns and coins, Spring
(After a Pompeian wall painting;
At the woman's unsubtle nipple the first lamb yawns)
As if they saw behind the scenes

Not the Discus Thrower, page 9 —
From a marble in the Palazzo Lancelotti —
Never that, no more, or the Greek boy with the jaculus,
      my own
Age, page 10;
                        I tossed it too but antiquity magnifies.
Inward or outward these eyes?

Eight of us that drank the air here.
Now joy is difficult (like Beauty), but the big tower would
      have us
Make our verse like his, sing
Jubilant Muses. And these sad quidnuncs
Sidling by and round some broken thing,

Avoiding commitment; some woman laid them
Low or they denied her, Mater Saeva
Cupidinum — what ode?
                                Some fellows sacked for her,
                                    plucked burning
After lights out from the sidereal bush
(In the haggard with a skivvy, in the hay)

Flagrante dilecto behind the fawnstoned ballalley
And sacked. What end to those fellows?
The bogmaidens walked away with some fine scalps.
(For the matter in an ode, to penetrate to
The great beat, thrown out, lost extra muros)

And these are husked, the flail is on them, unbuttoned
The only seamless garment, it is the dinginess
Hurts, affronts.
And Hermes (curvae lyrae parens) fashioning the toy
For love and the echoes of, for resonance;

Lynx lion tree-stumped, flamingo
Grounded by that lute, and the hells too in suspension,
Held up by a lover, Orpheus page 13,
Where the dead hung off like these from the barbarous
    new ghost
With all that sounding metaphor, like these, the lost

Who still drift in the old flesh, confusing the
Gods, who no longer sing to their own wires
Or hang together
In the beat that is one beat, the all-beat.
Eight we were in the fine young weather;

Bright flashes, and some gone down Earth's
Hollow foundations.
                    (That other Hermes, the conductor, what
Page, Psychopompus, with a soul for Charon's fishprow)
Time to go now, time to be on the way.
(That was a woman the winghatted God had in tow)

Reminding me of that old girl being led away
Half dead at the top and too much down below.
Graveclothes the heavy skirts she heaped up to her navel,
The raw focus of it, and they bundled her away,
Poor soul not down yet to the ultra violet ghost,

In the main Asylum grounds O years ago.
                            Edited by T. E. Page,
A prig but he did leave Faunus that field artillery.
Something came through,
A name, a coin, a winged horse,
Inked over by yours truly where they walk now,

The unburied,
Illustrating something, Limbo or something, the
        unregarded
Who underlie us.
                    Three measures
Of clay and we're at liberty to leave
To lay our tin wreaths on more iambic matter
At the Big Tower (those centenaries)
In Ballylee, Ballylee,
Through Loughrea and Kilchreest where my own kin lie
        strewn
In the all mothering weathering Galway skies,
To a dead swan in Leda's thighs.

63

YEATS'S TOWER AT BALLYLEE

> Is every modern nation like the Tower
> Half-dead at the top?
>
> W. B. YEATS

A pilgrimage is one slow foot
After the other, the agony of the heart
That looks to a place that will ripen like a fruit.
Yet I arrive in a Ford car
At the Tower talking of markets and wool
And corn drowned in the stook, the country around
Rain-rotten, the wet road buzzing like a spool
And trees at their year's end
Dropping the loaded sky to the ground.
I arrive talking of heifers and wool
And am confronted by the soul
Of a man in whom man cried like a great wound.

Somewhere a man will touch his image and burn
Like a candle before it. What happened here
In this ruined place of water and drowned corn
May still be here.
The oaken door hangs open, I go in
To a desolate underground that drips;
Shadows are on the stairs, the walls are weeping
A peacock paint, where a shoe slips
I clamber into a chamber like a tomb
Or a dim woodcut by William Morris
And suddenly I know the tower is
A boy's dream and the background of his rhyme.

Here where country blood was spilt
Neither earth nor stone cries out, for this is a dream-
    structure;

All that the brazen Norman built
To house a score of bullies in black armour
Deflected and turned to phantasy
By the boy who brooded on book and paint
Long mornings in his father's study
As mediaeval as a saint:
This is the Tower at last, its passion spent
And wearied of its own brutality
Where a boy could dream like Gabriel Rossetti;
Useless as verse and as magnificent.

I turn from the arty chimneypiece where glass
Has the pale wash of dreamy things and climb
Through a rude and navel arch, I pass
A sentry-go where no man turned a rhyme;
And the narrow stairway leads me to the place
Where he worked at the great table
Or lifted his tall height to pace
The enormous floor of his own fable;
Did he wear iron then, I wonder,
Or when the shadows stole the candle-light
Imagine himself all constellated night?
Il Penseroso in the magic chamber?

Yet nothing is here but the wind in the swinging windows
And the roar of the flood waters far below,
Not a house in sight, the corn in rows
Drowned and the drizzle rotting in the meadows:

The earth that cares for nothing but its seasons
Of lust and fruiting and death
Worked all about him here and gave no reasons
Why any man should waste his breath
In delicate definitions of a mild
World where man is the whole,
The individual soul
A heavenly cradle for the newborn child.

From the boy's dream to this reality
Of brutal weather and brutal stone
The Norman brought him. I come on the right day
To see for myself how earth can change a scene.
Rain and desolation, isolation
And fear in civil war can bring a man
To that harsh point in contemplation
Where soul no longer sees the sun:
In that bleak vision can man live,
Not summing up heaven and earth in measure?
Can he spend himself like a rich treasure
Where only the animal qualities survive?

Here at last he knew what opposites
War in one person. He became a man.
And the man divided into the primitive cross
Of two men in one rhythm. When the Norman
Came to the top the poet's words were blood
And what was good but a mere vision
Of arrogant foray, rape, and ride.
And then soul took its turn and with precision
Divined like an architect a house of life
Where violence had an energetic place
Only to find a holy face
Stare back serenely from the end of strife.

I climb to the wasting storey at the top.
His symbol's there where water and watery air
Soak through the plaster. The higher we clamber up
Into ourselves the greater seems the danger;
For the wider the vision then
On a desolate and more desolate world
Where the inspirations of men
Are taken by man and hurled
From shape into evil shape;
With the good and the grace gone out of them
Where indeed is there hope for men?
So every civilization tires at the top.

Around me now from this great height
Is a vision I did not seek. I have avoided it
And now I am forty-five
And wars blow up again, the east is lit,
Towns burn, villages are bombed,
With people everywhere in flight,
Their households on a handcart, or entombed
In homes that fell about them in the night,
And dragging children homeless in the air;
A mass migration of the humble
Before some war-mad general.
O the higher we climb up the wider our despair.

This tower where the poet thought to play
Out some old romance to the end caught up
The dream and the dreamer in its brutal way
And the dream died here upon the crumbling top.
I know the terror of his vision now:

A poet dies in every poem, even
As blossom dies when fruit comes on the bough,
And world is endless time in which things happen
In endless repetition, every man
Repetitive as a pattern, no soul
But the sprawling spirit of the whole
Massing upon the careless earth like frogspawn.

Everywhere is the world. And not less here
Because the stream, dividing, moats the place.
To live a fairy tale he bought this tower
And married a woman with a pleasant face;
And built in bookshelves, cupboards, hung
His pictures up and walked around
His beehive and his acre, wrung
Some civilization from the ground:
And yet instead of rhyming country ease
As in the eighteenth century we find
Him raving like a man gone blind
At the bloody vision that usurped his eyes.

Below me in the road two countrymen
Are talking of cattle and the price of wool,
Glad of the gossip and something held in common,
That scene would have been peaceful
An hour ago, but now I stumble down
In horror, knowing that there is no way
Of protest left to poet or to clown
That will enlarge his future by one day.
I could beat a policeman, bawl in a square, do gaol
For something silly. And what avails it? I
Step into the drizzle of the sky
Despairingly, to talk of the price of wool.

LETTER FROM BALLYLEE

Raftery, a tramp poet,
Sung for the thatches around the homespun girl
Whose name was Mary Hynes:
Later, of course, the beauty was debauched
By some hard-riding nameless
Country gentleman,
And died lost and wrinkled in
A bog cabin.

The girl goes always to the other fellow.
Exalt no girl, my friend;
Flesh no arrow. Witness this man who plumps anew
The old stone shell by the river.
Now he sings of God and lesser things
And studies planetary ebb and flow
Who saw Helen leave the high wall for
A quite ordinary lover.

He gets by, like
A hermit crab who blunders in from the blue
Bristle of the sea.
Waiting a new skin he hears
The old shell singing. Pitiful
The story, how an old love can discompose us.
Perhaps I should sing God too
And the partial planets, did this girl allow me
Who puts me at the disposal of the Muses.

DIALOGUE BETWEEN RAFTERY AND DEATH

Argument: Raftery the poet finds that his mistress, a married woman, is having an affair with a visiting sailor. The shock is severe and he considers death for the first time as a part of life. Tradition tells us that he saw the bony figure of death one night in his room; and that he who was blind found his sight while the vision lasted. He denied this vision later, however, under pressure from the clergy, and I prefer to take it as I write it here.

RAFTERY: There is some one here?
DEATH: Yes, Raftery.
RAFTERY: I know the voice.
DEATH: You know the voice.
RAFTERY: I do. It walks on all my drums. It fills me
Fuller than my heart. I have such noise
Inside me that the red rope of my pulse
Rocks me like a bell-tower. Visitor,
Are you inside or outside all my walls?
Are you Raftery's angel, that wild
trumpeter?
DEATH: No, Raftery. Never a trumpeter.
RAFTERY: Who, then?
DEATH: A Dignity that lacked a voice till this,
And so long silent, you may call me Silence.
RAFTERY: You use an alias so, for Silence is
The nightly gift this room gives Raftery.
You have another name?
I need not delve.
The steeple tops are still, yet toll it slowly
And all the clocks strike twelve.

You are an angel of death?
DEATH: Yes, Raftery.

RAFTERY :   A moment ago and I was throwing myself
             From every tower. Now strangely I find
                 dignity
             Inside me once again.
DEATH :   O, at the end it's natural
             For death to be received so quietly.
             I am so quiet myself, indeed, I invoke
             Quiet so palpable I leave it after me
             As you might leave the scent of tobacco
                 smoke.
             And, by the way, you smoke too much.

             Raftery looks up for the first time.
RAFTERY :   And you
             Are death?
DEATH :   Just your particular death.
RAFTERY :   I'm honoured, by God.
             I have a death the spit of Loss the Grocer.
DEATH :   Now, more respect —
RAFTERY :   O, all the pipes aboard
             Will shrill for the admiral. But I'll have a
                 death that looks
             Like Death and not like poor meek Loss,
                 whose sister
             Kept him collecting jumble clothes for blacks
             Till he, too, went in dread of the human
                 figure.
DEATH :   I am what you have let me be. I, Death, am
             The twin of Life, you know. With you we knit
             In one and make you a person. And a nasty
                 time
             I've had of it, my twin your favourite
             From the very first, never a thought for me;
             Always ignored. And the house never quiet.

You two jaunting, drinking, bringing women
    home
And singing, dancing, raving, ranting; every
    night
Bright as a brothel; no thought for a nice
    quiet tomb.

RAFTERY: I do not believe it.

DEATH: What?

RAFTERY: That you are Death.

DEATH: I insist that you believe in me, Raftery. You
    must
Allow me at least the dignity of existence.

RAFTERY: Death imposes more. The Striker. What!
    And the Strider of our dust.
The lightning flash, the thunder on the house.

DEATH: But I am — I mean I would be — I believe
    I could be
Thoroughly terrifying . . .

RAFTERY: Maybe to a mouse . . .

DEATH: But you ignore me, and give me no chance,
    Raftery.
I've lived like a prisoner — no, an exiled
    Royalty —
Inside you, Raftery; downcast, downtrodden
    because
You would not even become aware of me;
Why, tonight's the first time you have loaned
    me a face.
And what a face. Other men's deaths can
    wear
The loveliest frightful masks, but I have this
Parody as if you'd kicked my rear.
You are no gentleman, then a poet never is.

O, I was born unlucky. Give me a king
And I could be so vast and royal a shiver
All lamps would seek me out. A throne's the
        thing
For ghostly eminence. You've heard of
        Alexander
But never how night uncrowned him, how
        that Conqueror
Who'd so much sun he'd scorch a neighbour-
        ing hamlet
Was after dark but a star-and-gartered
        nightmare,
All the great Asian guttters running sweat.

RAFTERY :   You do not listen?
            Vanish, now, you interrupt me.
DEATH :   But you called me.
RAFTERY :   When?
DEATH :   You wished to die.
RAFTERY :   And God's grey footman ran obediently?
            Is a lover allowed no rhetoric? What if I
            did cry?
DEATH :   Must I leave emptyhanded?
RAFTERY :   Take me then. Or try.
DEATH :   You hold the ground
            Like a stone monument.
RAFTERY :   Do I hear you sigh?
DEATH :   I cannot move you.
RAFTERY :   Vanish, then, or not a sound.
            You interrupt my quarrel with the sky.
DEATH :   Another squabble with God? The old story
            Of your soul, that trouble-the-house. If you
                had not a soul,
            You'd still invent one, Raftery.

73

RAFTERY: Never. The soul ignites me
Like a spill of paper. Who'd be the fuel
Of a sky climber only to go on fire?
Soul burns everything, every love, it serves
My body worse than a syphilitic father,
A lunatic runs up and down my nerves.

Can't I love without Soul?
DEATH: Love. Love. Is the life principle
One vast erection, a candle in a windy cave?
You do not need this flary fellow . . .
RAFTERY: It is not sensible
To burn like this. Every woman's a grave,
And a corpse is all love needs. Yet Raftery
Is wrung by some tall lunar thing, wings beat
In heaven when he loves. O, Raftery
Has much too much of God for two clay feet.

I put the case to heaven. A man should walk
Untouched from woman to woman and take
      his pleasure.
My text is lechery . . .
DEATH: Jack Soul up his beanstalk,
God's glittering gossip . . .
RAFTERY: Every woman's a whore,
And lust is enough, for the pain when it
      aspires . . .
Distraction of moonlight, the donkey gallops
      around,
He brays from the grass, white rage to his
      flattened ears,
But the moon's no mare to be covered from
      the ground.

74

DEATH: You've taken up my theme and now you
        speak
        My life aloud. I'm the tired flesh inside
        Already muttering because trumpets break
        The lovely silence. The Soul will sound for
        pride,
        Go chiding, striding, in all its ignorance
        That we who're not combustible can tire
        Of wings and things and only ask the silence
        That lets us fall asleep about the fire.
RAFTERY: You are here still?
DEATH: Why, I'm stronger, now.
        Your flesh argues for me.
RAFTERY: Don't you know yet
        That every love invents me all anew?
DEATH: Nonsense. Your dreams unbuild you every
        night.
        You know you've too much wisdom to go on
        Enforcing Soul on the body, accumulating
        guilts
        For nothing. Why, even if you love this
        woman,
        She's only your death-wish walking round
        on stilts.

        I undermine you a little?
RAFTERY: I see you'll try
        Another tilt in a minute.
DEATH: I'm trying, now.
RAFTERY: I scarcely notice.
DEATH: Raftery, that is a lie.
RAFTERY: A little lie, perhaps. You've found some
        power
        You didn't have at first. It's not enough.

75

DEATH: But you're aware of me.
RAFTERY: I know you're here.
DEATH: The first black shadow. It's a curious stuff
             That tailors itself; it's Life's black underwear.

             I chill you a little?
RAFTERY: I stoke the fire
             Just that little more. Do you go away?
DEATH: I stay, of course. Your great Corrupter.
             From this time on I lend you my strange eye.
             A vision of acid, Raftery. You look upon
             A face and the face turns blank, the marvel-
                 lous living
             Mask collapses on the skeleton
             Before your eyes; and behind it — only
                 nothing.
RAFTERY: Against that nothing, I can think of a face
             That startles me, a woman's face that floods
             My whole house with sun and tall stained
                 glass . . .
DEATH: Against that nothing those few coloured muds
             Are less than nothing. And the moody woman
                 within
             Already knows the hands of a certain tailor
             And the garment he tailors, so she lives in sin
             And tries to forget him with a common sailor.
             But you know all this.
RAFTERY: I know it, O God.
DEATH: And still you live. And the sailor is still alive.
             For all your poetry and frenzy, poet,
             The seaman's got her. And still he is alive.
             How the Liberties will mock you over the
                 case.

	Mock you more than that poor man, her husband;
	The poet cast for a jockey of the high seas,
	A high-rigged boy with a bellyfull of wind.
RAFTERY:	I have no hangman's taste for certain neckwear.
DEATH:	A lovely instrument. One string finds all
	Silence in a note; an instrument for a lover
	Since all great love is suicidal.
	If you love greatly, then leave your love behind
	Fixed like a stone, your wildness in a gesture;
	Arrange it, Raftery, be forever self-contained;
	Death is the measure of a lover's stature.
	And the peace after the glory. To leave behind
	A self in people's minds . . .

RAFTERY: The glory is the slut's
Who could excite such passion, and for the
suicide
Peace is a burial with a stake down through
his guts.

DEATH: But someone must die for love. It should be
you
Who love love loudest.

RAFTERY: To sing love is my trade.
I'll go on singing if only to prove to you
A living poet is better than a dead.

RAFTERY: I see you no longer.

DEATH (*faint*): Do you mean, I can't be seen?

RAFTERY: You've gone.

DEATH:	I'm here, I'm here.
RAFTERY:	And scarcely to be heard.
	Have I finished you?
DEATH:	No. I'll be strong quite soon.
RAFTERY:	Soon enough, when I'm whiskered and grey-haired,
	A crutch in my hand and the priest beside my bed
	And no tall woman smiles at me from a poem.
	Where are you now?
DEATH:	I think I'm — once more dead.
RAFTERY:	Then let us call a general post-mortem.

RAFTERY'S DIALOGUE WITH THE WHISKEY

RAFTERY

If you shortened many a road and put a halo
On every thought that was growing in my head,
Have I not been to you as the brown nut to the hazel,
Your fruit, O my comrade?
And in many a lonely bed have I not praised you
With sleepy words no virgin ever heard?
And after all this, O the spite of it, here in Kilchreest
You topple a tallow candle and burn my beard.

Troy in its tall sticks never burned with a blaze
As bright as Raftery's hairs when that evil spark
Leaped on his skull and from that holy rooftree
Pitchforked his spluttering thatch;
Shame on you! not even Mercury who rose
Out of the cradle to fall on evil ways,
Stealing cattle, would hobble my wits and roast them
Hide and hair like that in the fire of my face.

O I was the sight then and the great commotion;
Wells running dry and poor people peeling their legs
With barrels and pails, and the fish flying down to the
       ocean;
And look at me now! a mere plaster of white of eggs!
Look at me! a bonfire to folly! but no man
Was ever saint till he was a sinner first;
And I'll break with you now though it cost me the
       mannerly company
Of the gay talkers who follow a thirst.

So I dismiss you. Here! Take your mouth from my
       mouth!

I have weighed you, O creature of air, and the weighman
    cries,
'Here's nothing will balance a holding of land in the south,
Beef on the hoof there and grass climbing up to the skies;
What's whiskey to hanging bacon?
To a glittering hearth and blue delphware?
Will it put a Sunday cost on any man,
I ask you, or leave him to walk bare?'

Ah, sweet whisperer, my dear wanton, I
Have followed you, shawled in your warmth, since I left
    the breast
Been toady for you and pet bully,
And a woeful heartscald to the parish priest;
And look! If I took the mint by storm and spent it,
Heaping on you in one wild night the dazzle of a king's
    whore,
And returned next morning with no money for a curer,
Your Publican would throw me out of the door.

THE WHISKEY

You blow hot and cold, grumbling,
The privilege of the woman and the poet.
Now let me advise you, Man of fancy stomach,
Carry a can and milk a nanny goat!
Drink milk! for I am not for you — as I am not indeed
For your brother the miser; but, ah, when the miser's heir
Grows into manhood and squanders I'll walk through the
    company
And call that man my dear.

I grow too heady now for your grey blood;
And you do little good to my reputation

With your knock-knees and themulous jowls — for God's
　　sake
Pay the tailor to press your pelt and tuck it in!
What can I be to you now but a young wife to an old
　　man?
Leave me to the roarers in the great universities,
The masters of Latin with the big ferules
Who know what use strong whiskey is!

Hush, now! I'll speak or burst. You have no pith,
And I pity the botch of a carpenter who planed you down.
You are maudlin at table ere the company is lit,
And among clowns, the heaviest clown.
I have given you pleasure, yet you round on me like a
　　lackey.
Who will swear he was overworked and underpaid;
And tomorrow, O most grievous insult of all, you'll repent
　　of me
That the priest may help you into a holy grave.

RAFTERY

Ah, that tongue was sharpened in many a bad house
Where candles are hooded on the black quays of the
　　world;
Many is the sailor it stripped to the bleak hose
And the Light Dragoon with his feather furled;
I hear it now and I pray that a great bishop
Will rise with a golden crook and rout you out of the land,
Yourself and the rising family of your sins,
As Patrick drove the worms out of Ireland.

You're an illness, a cancer, canker, a poison,
Galloping consumption, broken breath,
Indiaman's liver, thin diseases of the person,

Cholera Morbus and the yellow death;
You're the two sour women who wait here by my mattress
With Christian charity and broken hen-eggs
To mess my only features, but if I live to denounce you
I'll empty every tavern when I get upon my legs.

THE WHISKEY

If hard words broke bones every sad rascal
With a bleached tongue who turns on me of a morning
Would have done for me long ago, yet I rise again like
    the pasch
Quietly, brightly, in their minds and they return.

RAFTERY

Who returns but the shiftless drifters, the moon's men?
Stray calves who'd suck at any udder?
Waifs, bagmen, beggars, and an odd fool of a lord
Crazy enough not to know better?

THE WHISKEY

Men of merriment, the wide girthed men
Whose eyes pen cattle, and slender men who hold
The curves of a filly together with one finger
While the other strips an heiress of her gold;
Equal those, O Fiddler, men of the great gay world
Who can dance a stately figure or bow prettily to a queen
And keep fine manners though the blood be rearing
Like a red stallion on the fair green.

RAFTERY

Blackguards, rakes, who rise up from cards
Only when the sun is trumped there on the table
Like the red ace of hearts, take them, the gamblers
Who wouldn't pay their debts were they able;

Dicers, procurers, who'll give you an I.O.U.
On the honour or dishonour of a wife or daughter,
Take them, the lot of them, hog, devil, or dog,
And drown them in a bucket of bog water.

THE WHISKEY

Poets and musicians —

RAFTERY

and absentee landlords,
Militiamen on hayfeet — strawfeet who burn
Brightly as red lamps in a lanewife's back parlour,
Taking, as always, the wrong turn;
I leave you to them and to the landlord's agent
Who shivers beside you day-in day-out
Walled in by the hostile murmurs of the rainy grasslands
In an old windy house.

THE WHISKEY

For a homespun poet whose pride I nursed
When doors were shut on him and dogs barked at his
        heels,
Your gratitude is such I'll swear a cutpurse was your
        father
And your mother the lady who tied eels.
Desert me, indeed? You windy bag of old words,
You wan wizened weasel with one worn tooth!
If I whistled tomorrow you'd hobble to me on your sores;
And that's the truth.

RAFTERY

Whistle, then!

THE WHISKEY

                        I'll whistle when
I'm in the mood.

RAFTERY

Whistle! Whistle!

THE WHISKEY

Maybe when you've money and can spend,
When you're a farmer slaughtering the poor thistle,
Stoning crows or coaxing cows,
Counting your corn grain by grain,
With thirteen bonhams to every one of your sows,
And you carrying a big purse at the fair.

RAFTERY

Good-bye for ever then!

THE WHISKEY

Good-bye Raftery.

RAFFERTY

I'll never be a farmer.

THE WHISKEY

                And where is the need?
Poetry and whiskey have lived always on the country.
Why wouldn't they indeed?

RAFTERY

You're right. Why shouldn't I tax the heavy farmer?
I give him wit. And you? You give him — what?

THE WHISKEY

No matter. We are two necessary luxuries.

RAFTERY

Listen! I'll drink to that.

MARY HYNES

(After the Irish of Raftery)

That Sunday, on my oath, the rain was a heavy overcoat
On a poor poet, and when the rain began
In fleeces of water to buckleap like a goat
I was only a walking penance reaching Kiltartan;
And there, so suddenly that my cold spine
Broke out on the arch of my back in a rainbow,
This woman surged out of the day with so much sunlight
I was nailed there like a scarecrow,

But I found my tongue and the breath to balance it
And I said: 'If I bow to you with this hump of rain
I'll fall on my collarbone, but look, I'll chance it,
And after falling, bow again.'
She laughed, ah, she was gracious, and softly she said
     to me
'For all your lovely talking I go marketing with an ass,
I'm no hill-queen, alas, or Ireland, that grass widow,
So hurry on, sweet Raftery, or you'll keep me late for
     Mass!'

The parish priest has blamed me for missing second Mass
And the bell talking on the rope of the steeple,
But the tonsure of the poet is the bright crash
Of love that blinds the irons on his belfry,
Were I making an Aisling I'd tell the tale of her hair,
But now I've grown careful of my listeners
So I pass over one long day and the rainy air
Where we sheltered in whispers.

When we left the dark evening at last outside her door,
She lighted a lamp though a gaming company
Could have sighted each trump by the light of her un-
     shawled poll,

And indeed she welcomed me
With a big quart bottle and I mooned there over glasses
Till she took that bird, the phoenix, from the spit;
And 'Raftery', says she, 'a feast is no bad dowry,
Sit down now and taste it!'

If I praised Ballylea before it was only for the mountains
Where I broke horses and ran wild,
And not for its seven crooked smoky houses
Where seven crones are tied
All day to the listening top of a half door,
And nothing to be heard or seen
But the drowsy dropping of water
And a gander on the green.

But, Boys! I was blind as a kitten till last Sunday.
This town is earth's very navel!
Seven palaces are thatched there of a Monday,
And O the seven queens whose pale
Proud faces with their seven glimmering sisters,
The Pleiads, light the evening where they stroll,
And one can find the well by their wet footprints,
And make one's soul;

For Mary Hynes, rising, gathers up there
Her ripening body from all the love stories;
And, rinsing herself at morning, shakes her hair
And stirs the old gay books in libraries;
And what shall I do with sweet Boccaccio?
And shall I send Ovid back to school again
With a new headline for his copybook,
And a new pain?

Like a nun she will play you a sweet tune on a spinet,
And from such grasshopper music leap
Like Herod's hussy who fancied a saint's head

For grace after meat;
Yet she'll peg out a line of clothes on a windy morning
And by noonday put them ironed in the chest,
And you'll swear by her white fingers she does nothing
But take her fill of rest.

And I'll wager now that my song is ended,
Loughrea, that old dead city where the weavers
Have pined at the mouldering looms since Helen broke
    the thread,
Will be piled again with silver fleeces:
O the new coats and big horses! The raving and the
    ribbons!
And Ballylea in hubbub and uproar!
And may Raftery be dead if he's not there to ruffle it
On his own mare, Shank's mare, that never needs a spur!

But ah, Sweet Light, though your face coins
My heart's very metals, isn't it folly without pardon
For Raftery to sing so that men, east and west, come
Spying on your vegetable garden?
We could be so quiet in your chimney corner —
Yet how could a poet hold you any more than the sun,
Burning in the big bright hazy heart of harvest,
Could be tied in a henrun?

Bless your poet then and let him go!
He'll never stack a haggard with his breath:
His thatch of words will not keep rain or snow
Out of the house, or keep back death.
But Raftery, rising, curses as he sees you
Stir the fire and wash delph,
That he was bred a poet whose selfish trade it is
To keep no beauty to himself.

THE SMALL TOWN OF JOHN COAN

I

Invent them for us,
The open storeys overhead: we need
Them, the overplus, the changing
Bodies and a new seed.

Let Olympus overhang the street
And gossips will be poets. I want to see
Cornuted bulls, and amorous
Birds in the family tree.

Strict biology
Caters to no truth we need. Who hid
In Juno's robe
Begat a god

And time and things like towns
That burned famously and battles that would yield
Hubbub and talk enough
For any man in a field:

Give us the lady's name
Who hides in the golden shower; boredom
Is where we lie now, with never a window
On Messalina's Rome;

And the sad river never
Manages to be Cydnus, never will float
Even in dream pharaoh's
Daughter or gilded boat.

Amoris domina, saddle this
Golden ass to break through to the tale
Of new dimensions;
Mother of love, command another Fall,

New Eve, new Adam, a new tree,
Gardens where nymphs are
Stories of air and water; let there be
Pipes in the air,

The cobble break
Into the blue, the town tumble into apple
Blossom, the Graces nude and linked
Lead out the season in a dancing rabble.

II
And just when he was all in it,
From head to foot the welling heartbeat,
This thing, this town, ceased to articulate for him.
Some ogre behind the font?
Some field god tired of making wheat?

Shocked when a child sister
Was walked in her deadbox to the old church
He saw the light turn sinister:

Some one had moved the morning
With an almost visible lurch
And set it down askew.

Afterwards certainly all world was
Out of the true
Morning after morning.

III

Semele's son
Squandered to the riot buds in a field,
His privates blown, a no-man
Dowsed and spelled:

The unplotted torso swells; in the round
Of the year he rolls, reason enough for those
Revolving set-pieces; and in demand,
Season burgeoning from season; every woman his.

Autre temps.
              What so eager happens now?
What neighbour hill is begging me to die,
Offering endless resurrections?

Now spring is harnessed to a commonplace,
What rose glows in Cancer? What boy's face
In the empty stubble can autumn contemplate?

IV

The portrait of Mrs O
Overall is black with
One eye bead sunken in
A beaked shawl.

The eye's the thing, receiver of
Dismembered cities if needs be. There
The town is
Upside down in the harsh indifferent glare.

She broods in sombre areas; pruned
To crucifixions are the trees in her garden;
She stands on all the ways out in some

Survival like rock, won't go
Into water colours ever; simply shares
Her matter with some old-fashioned status quo.

V

And I on the Alley bridge
Unjointing the rod that evening, summer
Aloft and alow and
All the old ones out in Abbey Row

When behind me up she rears
In her daffodil jumper, her
Whoring number, and she peers into my fishbasket
Low, low.

Pisces two.
        Some are dead
Who mumbled into her buttercups, gone down
The darling men, the King's very own:

And she offers so freely now that ardent lap
It's said, O sad mishap, the lovers' tree
On River walk has even got the clap.

MARIS STELLA

I

In the flat glaze of the quays,
On wet stone where evening lies, the fishermen
Overhaul their gear.

And the light receives
Blue overalls and black rubber boots
And drowns them sometimes in a wintry flash
From which they recover themselves, fastened by the
usual thoughts
To the bobbing floats of their familiar heads,
And find again their own appearances.

Around them always is the sea:
And inside them with no murmur over the ground
The sea; and below, how do I know
How many fathoms down
Their trailing limbs go?
Into what fishtailed memory?

Seas in their heads, too; do they turn
Over in their beds with every ebb and flood?
Their sleep wide-open weather
Where fish swim and birds cry
Over and around them and inside them forever?

So not as men only but living up and down
Their obscure spirals of air and water they
Add their little rhythms to the sea,
Each man an estuary.

Yes, almost unhumanly,
Almost finned and winged as fish and fowl,
Almost as certain as they
In their own elusive counterpoint they move out,
Not to collide with but to ride
All rhythms and forces
As centaurs, horses themselves, ride horses.

But so incessantly
Do they need to retrieve themselves from drowning
In boats, in thoughts, in seas outside and in, however,
They become aware, they know terror
As the other pulse, the greater.

And they dare not eavesdrop on themselves, they dare
Not look within where all the underworld
Is turning into myth
In lust and dream, in drama and in terror,
All that they are
To utter you who are unutterable:
You, caught up like a breath,
The very last before death.

II

Men with meanings
Inside that wait like cold wicks in oil,
Here they endure the wide stare of things
Roosting like seabirds, here they pull
Themselves out of the waters to keep station
On you like some continuous intimation:
Do you know them from other birds who fold their wings
Above the coasts and rain down droppings?

Are you always arriving ashore
And through them up some old waterstairs of feeling?
Are you the Igniter who climbs up the tower
Of their gaze to light that archaic reeling
Lanthorn in each face?
Are you that cold thing in the gaze?
That barbarous look of the older climate,
The halfmade man, the not-yet-private?

The fisheaters, the fishcatchers
Who rise arrayed in and shedding fishes like
Electric shocks, who disappear for days into the weathers
Of the giant's house, but to ride
Out when all is lost to dodge upon
An immense and dangerous horizon
And only when we've lost all hope
Come home on a fair wind up the telescope?

III

LOVE POEM

It was not difficult for Blake: they gossiped
Daily, reality and he. But I,
A poet, too,
Find it the bodily thing outside the body,
Yet near it, like a wound upon the thigh.
And so I seek you
Like pain; and when like pain you've slipped
Over my borders again, there's still this lack.
Heaven's up a strut and I'm no steeplejack.

And where's the communion? You with a tailored God
Neatly made to measure, who will sit
Inside and share
A woman's world all day and talk of it:
And yet with a look the whole tall stick is lit
And your head of hair
Becomes an adventure far above your head.
I know it, I, who never walked down the street
Like Blake, but took a cushion to your feet.

THE ANIMATE

Her mirror told her once it was
A mistake not to be beautiful:
And something ebbed away from her.
But as her face diminishes
And almost as flesh vanishes,
Nerve living on nerve until
I can see her naked will,
Her intense skeleton discloses
The most unaccountable of roses.

On this top rock a wintry and rough
Wide plaque of sea-sky does not dull
Your delicate and deliberate reds:
You know that life is to the tough
And that your inches are enough
To show what is incalculable —
Love that makes the mirror tall
And gives you the image that you sought,
Thighs that tower beyond thought.

LAKSHMI

A sheet of paper, placed
Over this dangerous bronze figure,
Covers up the East
And the dancer's narrow waist,

India gone, sunken
The archaic shining knot; white paper
Is the churned-up ocean
That cast her upwards, buttocks in motion,

Helmeted hair, enormous
Ear-rings and all, the necklace
In sacred circles; There was
Dancing here that folded into a lotus.

The bare breasts still now, the nubs
At rest, but the twisted rhombs
Of the hips still echo
Temple gongs.

The belly is so young
And the undented navel. Instruments
Should sound like this,
Keeping distance

Like the long arm that falls to the gathering fingers,
Hand sinister, that knows space
Is precious and must not spill.
The two legs are tough with grace —

And since they are the bearers, yield nothing
To immodest silks, who must tower
Up from their native earth
To carry a little flower

Where, coppered above
The heartbeat, on its fine meridian floats
A face flawed with neither age or youth;
Here Ganges pours

But merely rounds the bud
She contemplates, that must not dwindle;
On her right hand it rides, and earth
Turns quietly on the spindle.

THE POEMS OF LOVE

All the poems of love are one;
All women too. The name that runs
Profanely between love and lover
Is the name repeated over
In the rosaries of nuns.
All the poems of love are one.

Solar red, masochist black,
There's precedent for each in heaven;
Whatever be a body's leaven
The rosaries of the holy nation
Thrill to some transfiguration.
Love makes up the thing we lack.

All the women Tom and Jack
Buy or bed, the slumtown tits,
Have bright otherworld habits;
A queen shares pillows with a clown,
Still nebulously wears her crown,
And is most royal on her back.

When Tom and his hedge mistress come
Drunken to the judgement seat,
The obscene measures on his tongue
Start the heavens into song;
Endlessly must Tom recite
The love he made by rule of thumb.

And brawling face and bawling gums
Fade fawnlike into some young grace;
Love lives serenely many ways;
Love lives in all that it may not lack
Its body in riots, drunks and drums
And the rosaries of nuns in black.

RIVER LANE

I

That girls in the river, nymphs
Aloof in the female whorl and seashell shiver,
Could ever become old women beating clothes!
That those gay whipsters, virgin born
Tuning the milkwhite unicorn
Under the singing linnet at lane doors
Should turn to old mad gossips thumb to nose.

That our Madge who had such bubble and bud
Into her latest motherhood,
Forgetting that the body's lent,
Should prolong the happy time of rut,
A great bulldozing Bacchic slut,
All anguish when her time was spent,
Still clinging to her instrument;

All the passions come to stay;
In love or out of it no holiday.
With little left, the wick is all.
Ridiculous Helen will blue the moon
With the shadow of her going down;
Leda in her dotage scull
A mess of feathers on a pool;

And our old drunken Madge sail out
To bully the babble in the common street;
In the square no less, filled with the itch
And opulence of the vanished myth,
And suffering some kind of death,
Shake her clothes off every stitch
To show the roses of the bitch.

What lover ever who threw on this peg
A coat of arms could sing the wagging dug,
Or see the seaborne for the crows,
Or know for truth that on this breast
Man runs, a vast historic beast,
His race between her mouth and knees
And shoots his arrows at her skies?

Precisely under the church clock
She spins for all eyes round the Zodiac.
The world stands still
While she unlocks the raven hair
In the lost youth that envelops her.
Percussion of pigeons on the chapel bell:
The town one worldwide windowsill.

A little quiet country place
Shattered by an old mad mask of savage face;
Venus Anadyomene
Gone screwy, with every churchman's shaft
Feathering her broomstick tuft;
Careless of councils and decrees
The pigeons flutter round her knees.

She has the square to herself,
Old Madge, fallen off the waggon, and off the shelf
Where the cruise of oil is rich
With the Virgin's face, and history is not
The crescent that grows and ranges round the lot
To finish its moon round such,
Occulting on a cratered crutch.

Yet a most sonorous whore;
An excess of flesh; the epic had its hour.
And now like bats she calls her twittering dead
To beak and nuzzle, the horsed Huzzar
Or maybe her first conqueror,
That Esquire in his hunting red
Who drank from her uplifted head.

II
Piously
They say; a Rosary
In the flagrant hands; the treed God
On the gargantuan deserted mamillae:

From her house of finches,
Shouldered by six goes
Her piece of pine;
We take it in turn, each man to his trick:

She's rights in the old graveyard, so
It's round the town for us, an ancient custom;
My right shoulder aches at the stone cross;
The old drumbeat was a weight;

And I doubt if she's yet translated
From that batwinged virago, akimbo
In her bawling shawl;
The gates are open and we trample in

Where the de Burghs lie under broken
Slabs. Glass wreaths
Crunch on unkempt graves. It's noon
When we reach her upturned pile and pay her down.

Not a sob, not a face breaks; she'd gone
Far past her span, gone on, gone on
With the untimely rhetoric
Of a mastodon.

The first spadeful; a shake
Of holy water from a naggin bottle,
A Pater and Ave. (Though she died in a Mary habit
Nobody thinks she'll make it)

Noon, and in the spare woodwork
Of December, low
As a lilac blooms suddenly the sun;
And I think maybe she did and all:

For what man ever
Quite totted up the human figure?
Here's famous holy ground at least,
And she lies at long last with the great.

THE RIVER WALK

Disturbing it is
To take your stick sedately talking,
Evening in the water and the air,
And discover this; that a woman is a river.
The mythic properties are hard to bear.

Dismaying are
The ways she will intrude — if she intrude
Or merely assume the garments that you give her:
But a water willow stared at for so long
Glows graciously and knows the why you brood.

And such gesticulation —
Are you so young? — before the gentle birch
In its first shimmer: Lover, are you true
To one, or merely finding all you search
Brings the one woman home to you?

But how absurd to see
Her in that stilted bird, the heron in
A silt of river, all her blues pinned up:
In that brocaded goose the swan
For all her myths with Jupiter on top.

Dangerous, dangerous
This mythology. The doctors know it
And reason of it now like any poet.
Lover, go back no farther than your birth:
A woman is a woman, not the earth.

Her human business is
To resolve a man of other women always,
Not be, in a beautiful grotesque, all bodies
So various, a lover — if the girl insist
On love — must be a very pantheist.

A PUBLIC APPOINTMENT

He was stranding on the ripple
When she looked, the virgin. Her mute maids stood
Broadbeamed in the morning, washed, and nude as ingots,
While she went on.
The thing before her was no monstrous shell,
But a red man run over by the ocean.

She was to learn that pity was a pity
Between a man and a woman, but could she then, a virgin,
Know it, whose body heavenly Athene
Used so subtly
To break down this bull-man to her own
Particular lust — that's beyond flesh and bone?

So what the hero saw
In his run-down vision while his footsteps ranged
Around him uncontrollably as dolphins,
Was the white tower she was
And the sacred woman
In the city inside the city, unsacked Ilium.

Lustres he'd lost at sea
Would come back, he'd borne such brunts before
On his wide sea-front and taken them for granted;
But this was a new peril,
And in his weakness sweeter than the Siren,
This pity she offered him, so sisterly, so virgin.

The first look had made them
All ever they could be to one another,
Suppliant to Goddess, son to mother;

Neither was aware
Of all that was lost
Though it wept and swooned around them in the ghost.

And the girl had felt
The male in the storm that breached him, the rough pelt
Of the lover, and all the rolling bed.
But the man was down
Below the mercury; undone.
The great boomerang remained unthrown.

So Pallas Athene had her way.
Ulysses, recovered from the ocean and the blue
Barbarous tattoos of the receding god,
Was returned posthaste
To his public appointment. All
In heaven and earth bow down to protocol.

Yet when his people, shepherds
With heads in the clouds and sailors pouring water,
Demanded a statue to that sacred eloquence,
What rose up in the square
Was not oracular, no great mouthing of stones,
But the wanderer, that slender buffeted bronze.

Yes, though he died old and slowly
Into his vineyards, requiring like the sun
One whole horizon to decline upon,
The image that remains
Is the haunted man on the main of love, forever
Sailing, and beside him a virgin at the tiller.

FIRST LOVE

And so it arrives, the moment
Of moments; not much to it, yet.
A pale pigtail of a moment,
The look not even languorous, nor the poise
Very delicate:
Little to indicate the torment
To come, or the woman in the girl's disguise;
A moment, even, that a boy can forget
And if he does remember it
Will find it is the stir in every story;
As if that Goddess, in a shiver from the sea
With her birth-bud trailing, but tall in a fleeting wet
Uncertain glory,
Made all his memory her mythology.

And already they are enemies;
Each seeking the thing not to be had,
A mirror for the eyes
And the larger equation of the self that is
Not balanced in a bed;
Nothing here to indicate the sighs
To come or tell them that whether they kiss
Or do not kiss the heart and head
Start their journey to the dead.
The thing she will remember will not vex
Her housekeeping, but he stands where the decks
Are stacked. Be careful of this equation, lad;
Unbalanced X
In all its powers is another sex.

EVENING OFF

Naked down to the maker's name,
Warranted, nubile,
The well-women, the famous Nine in their dance,
Have nothing on this girl in appearance:
They the lovely words of mouth;
She the bubble of dense youth.

For the rest, they drive;
And she, the driven,
Knows the new coat she wears is not her own
Opinion of herself; she put it on
As something that might happen her
With these, the high tight shoes that hurt her.

Ladies, you, too,
Sometime did likewise:
Or your heavy mothers, fresh from outfarms, did;
Go easy with tongue and stare, she does but add
Something from her own rainbow
To what she sees in the shop window.

And if she offends —
Leading round as she does
Her afternoon off, like a cow with one horn
She cannot park, it is difficult to be born;
Yourselves know that journey
From nothing to identity.

Leave ill to the witch-face
Watching her from the lane-mouth;
This girl's time will come, the illtime; Now the bells say
Sweet high-up and distant: 'Dear Dulcibella!'

The great belly will come;
But now she wears her latest letter home.

Purely she tells
Herself from those heel-stilts
That wobble to mother, father; and still she sees
That boy at the corner straighten up his knees:
Speak, Ladies, tell how
Everything, anything, happens to her now.

Tell her this knobbly young
Hairslick with the fag end on his tongue
Unfolding from his corner in a look
So townwise will be all her luck and crook:
Time strung like a guitar
The dear bells so sweet and far.

SUNDAY MORNING

If I make way for bells on Sunday morning,
Demure, deep in
Her Sunday hat she'll walk, tipping the tall
Flowering shrub, a lilac, at
The corner
Turning into Mespil Road.

A street new from the font, an old
Arrow of canal
Mounted, tufted by an ancient swan, is leading
Somewhere;
My bible woman hardly knows
The way she goes.

She carries the total injury of me;
In jeopardy. Almost
Rural the scene with elm and planetree, sun
At summer hoist, a wisp
Of smoke from some pedestrian;
Her penitent feet will lead her on.

She does not dally by the sluice
Or the resting barge. An odd head
Hangs on the bridge at Baggot Street;
God is dead,
His shadow what I throw far
Beyond into hurt and metaphor.

The whole world can see the lover's hands
Upon her. In the din
Of sweet bells she rises to confess
The evil bruise;
Hears another gospel start
In the regions of the heart;

What penitence can she profess?
How burn away
Back into her first
Girl-simile
The garden fallen around her, simple trees
Lovers and enemies?

WOMEN

I

The pity of it. Not to love
All the love we lean upon;
Always to be at some remove,
Always to be drawn
Towards the overwhelming one
We must meet alone.

O loneliness. We are born to them:
As mothers they mother us;
We break the navel chord like a limb
That as lovers they may love us:
But recover us
And leave them for our loneliness.

II

Rest, says the earth. And a woman delicately
Says 'it is here, it is in my arms somewhere'
But a woman is a lie
And I have a tower to climb, the tower of me,
And a quarrel to settle with the sky
But 'rest' says the woman, 'o lean back more;
I am a wife and a mother's knee,
I am the end of every tower.'

CONSUBSTANTIALITY

If heredity
Indeed determine history,
Helen, through her known bird's blood and Troy sticks
Burning, could well account herself the Phoenix.

But how shall I guess
At my father at all and his business
If I know only my mother and the long griefs
Of her four beautiful green leaves?

What shall I know of him, my milk-teeth won
At your quiet paps, unless I follow on
As the caterpillar clambers through his own rings
Suddenly to come on wings?

If father's thumb need
Luck or not, his image, a large dream, haunts his seed;
This kinship then is the blood's philosophy
And, followed, home, enlarges me.

I admit your motherhood —
My mouth is sweet with it — but is the male blood
And mind to be denied which also I inherited,
And your great lover discredited?

Then, bid me, Lady,
Stretch my boy's to a man's body,
And finding the new huge trick,
Engage you in a larger rhetoric.

For there's no glory in a house,
Where the master's absent, if his son's a mouse
Among the spinning wheels; think of my shame
If one day he came home

Out of the sea's tumult roping
The heaven's great song ashore, and I moping
Among the spitting suitors at the fire,
Field and cupboard nearly bare.

Could I offer in excuse
This love that makes me envious
Of time, the slow great stream, because it floats
Your murmuring wide leaves and drifts with your roots,

When this love so disperses me
Like vague air over your vegetable scenery
To tell like little steeples the sweet innumerable names
Of your small cities in my hazy palms?

No. Let the great bright bow
Stand upon the cloudy wall and bid me go
Seek him through blood and sweat, and fashion from the
        way
An heroic body for the Judgement day.

Lest, when the bow is bent,
He not recognise me in that summary moment
And I go down, too, with the rest before the whistling
        string,
A nothing to drift in nothing.

I must be about his business
For he comes so near my earth our various substances
Seem one, as trembling from the dim cocoon
The butterfly is dazzled leaf and sun.

BROTHER TWIN

One lagging his old bones
Against the winter wind in Connacht
Herds sheep and listens
To the other side:
'The Boddhisvatta Manjusri
Is the master of transcendental wisdom'.

The other, shaven twin
In the empty begging bowl of the East,
Wakens on a stupa, the holy dead forgotten,
Saying: 'The soft West
Is arriving on the sheepwalks, tomorrow
The lactation of ewes'.

The ram's groom relaying the fertile thing
Dies for a moment, new grass
Forgotten, showery Phallus
No weather king:
'The fifth station is that of a Boddisvatta,
No turning back'.

In the famine yawns the saintly twin:
'Nothing dies, not even
Man's dream of woman;
All night she walks, the honey drips, the sky
Is one great eye. In Galway now
A girl destroys infinity.'

Flushed from the female, turning over, brother
Sings to his opposite: 'Outrageously
Made of seven precious substances
Is the Bodhi-tree;

And they squat there accomplishing each sign,
Manjusri as Manjughosha on a lion,

Buddhas beyond recall, their
Dialogue done.
Hang up the skeleton. What chores delight us?
What women intervene?'
Manjusri's attributes are book and sword:
His too the tall blue lotus.

IV

IF GODS HAPPEN

If Gods happen
Only when we throw our wild unreasonable
Desires into a kind of definition,
Are they us? And are we then illimitable?

And always journeying
Vastly through ourselves, with every start
A new discovery of that great thing
Inside the heart?

A god happening
When we have talked ourselves out of the little city
We have inhabited too long.
And space is our necessity?

Happening, yet old as if left over
From another world; when things finitely bid us
Be infinite, do we discover
In us or in a god the end of our neurosis?

For One is always there
As if a journey ended, and all longing
Had formulated Him, indefinite and clear,
New, and oh the release, the self-delighting.

Our arrival towering
On the new beaches, old steeples and discontent
Lost, and our eternal talking
Drowned in the statement of a continent.

How large then this little beat
Of blood, this small dynastic pulse that throws
Such colonies out beyond all wit
And walls, this heart no taller than a rose?

THE CHRISTMAS VIGIL

Wherever else the real miracle
Was happening, with climates curtsying
To the small holy city, out here
On the west periphery
Our Galway weather hadn't nodded east.

Elsewhere the nub
And circles of rejoicing heaven, stars high and low
Lifting to the skyline
The figures of donkey, man and virgin
Moving towards Bethlehem.

So, on the old cart
Bumping on the road by Lopdells, today
Had not arrived, the trees
With aboriginal arms still making
Yesterday's rain

From the day's soft grey substance; no
New magnitude in the stone
Fields, no distances starting to flow
Into rainbows; there was only this
Same old world with yesterday's leftovers.

All the way to Mountbawn, with
Bullocks in a horned frieze staring
Egyptian from the roughmasoned gateways, ours
Storming the cart as we appeared;
We tossed them their turnips and went wheeling

Over the usual earth. Obviously
Christmas had not come to the brutes on this
Waterhaunted ledge of the Atlantic. It
Was quiet in the lambing paddocks, the ewes
Waiting at the troughs

In sops of gold straw for the broken oats;
And we dished it out, we two
Shepherds of sorts though no sky would open
For Nicholas Moran pipe in mouth now
And quite happy in his wingless span

Of Galway clay. Me too, for miracles belong
Over the ultimate horizon; nothing here
Has learned the rudiments,
No beast of ours
Drizzling over his fat roots will turn celestial,

Unlike the Bible ox
In the crib under the organ gallery, where
With a star strung like a kite above
And the new lunation in its eye,
The beast lights up with human love.

But this is the mystery welling
Up from some inner world in a sort
Of perennial heartbeat. All day the glow of it
Fills the back of my mind; but I won't look;
Not yet

Being simply afraid of what could happen.
I like things as they are,
World as it is, the wonder just round the corner;
And if at midnight
All the clocks in the world meet to chime

Over the world's newest child, this
Will be the more spacious for happening in my sleep
Where ends can meet in peace
When the great harps sweep out upon the pediments
And the wren waken with a tiny cheep.

VIRGIN

I

The Lady who intervenes
In the Trinity assumes
Her rights on a side altar,
A great wick that no flame lames
In a quiet arch of candle flames.

And over the dim paving
Where drowned lights are stepping stones,
In the cave of the nave,
Soled with silence that stir like water
Or whispers of prayer the women falter.

Slowly, glimmering
One after one for a moment in that still arch
Each putting a penny in the money box,
Each lights a candle and burns there
As if she'd set it to her hair.

Then one after one each woman grows
Anonymous;
They pass and are the past;
O sighing history
Shuffling by that knee!

Candles will die for their small
Concepts of virginity but she
Older than the vine sits always in the sun
Turning on all the one face
Full of grace.

Moon to what sun?
Mother of one Son
Shall I turn my back upon you and walk out?
Ere I with women find you inside me —
A tree, a growing reverie?

A great reverie
Drinking a thousand roots in me,
Growing till it opens my skull, Who then
Will gather me up
When I flower at the top?

II

Her hands are not tangible;
Her face drifts; and over all
Her body is the quality of distance
And the shine of water.

If guesses were gods,
How they would stride out towards her, seven leagues in
    each boot!
If gods are guesses, I am still moderate
In thinking they'd reach heaven through her thought.

How the heavens depend on her!
If her weather altered it would mean
Angels and their wide glories would drip from the air,
Melting in a bright shower round her like rain.

How be intimate with this
Translucent Atlas? Yet sometimes I awake
Softly as if I had been kissed
And blessed, to feel the earth quake.

MATER DEI

In March the seed
Fell, when the month leaned over, looking
Down into her valley.
And none but the woman knew it where she sat
In the tree of her veins and tended him
The red and ripening Adam of the year.

Her autumn was late and human.
Trees were nude, the lights were on the pole
All night when he came,
Her own man;
In the cry of a child she sat, not knowing
That this was a stranger.

Milk ran wild
Across the heavens. Imperiously He
Sipped at the delicate beakers she proffered him.
How was she to know
How huge a body she was, how she corrected
The very tilt of the earth on its new course?

ASSUMPTION

Some Syrian rainmaker
Invoking a minor image of power found her
Intrude, O enormous magic, and his hands
Dissolve in showers over many lands;
Earth turned woman, or woman into earth, he
Left this wild image to Syrian sorcery.
But O how they tamed her, the Greeks, the civilising
Mythologising Alexandrian schoolmen
And the soft Italians with the Christian eyes
Who ferried her over the tideless Mediterranean;
The muted breasts, the quiet, and on the top
A face bright as a waterdrop.

Assumed into heaven, she,
A statue among statuary,
Consumes in her single fire the line
Of barbarous virgins who dwelt between
Trinities in their season.
Heaven and earth are in division;
The gross fertilities, the ram, the bull,
Left out-of-doors while in her shuttered parlour
When she bares the nipple
No rye rises, no wheaten flower;
Only her dreams stir
The peacock presences of air.

This mild lady
Calms the gross ambitions with a steady
Country look. No drums, no dances,
No midnight fires, no sacrifice of princes;
She takes her pail among the cows
And bolts her fowl in the fowl house;

Evoe, if the sun-headed god is gone, there's still
The house to be done, white linen hung
Upon the hedge. The serene axle
Goes round and round in a crucifixion,
But earth is a pot of flowers. Foreign tongues
Commune above her in a drift of wings.

BRIGID HER EVE
For Nancy and Conor and a rush Cross

Origins are
Swamps and rush cradles, so never
Mind me if I see
You as no lady but barbarous and
Maybe beautiful, as when
The scurf of winter grass in Galway
Ignites to light or
Rain and you are nothing less
Than metaphor

That I do not care to
Resolve ever and won't ever bother to
Catch close and make small like
Another woman or even
A tower of ivory or house of Gold, thus
Missing out on major things like weather
And distances that touch
Other distances right round this
Only and mighty orb

I know the feel of
Up through my legs since
I staggered erect from the
Tremors of trees, in which you
Were a bark skirt and a
Dogbite of roses, most fecund for
A boy lover. And you, do not
Come closer either, for there is
Nothing nearer.

Just simply be;
Continuing, with my own bit
Of history evaporating while
I find big things in consonants, like the
Discovery of a spring well, or
The hunch of a spring plough on the first headland
When all the world was a vowel;
Big things like lost continents;
Something that has your style,

Or lack of style,
Like the raw bulb of the ewe that leaves
A lamb on the green, or the
Tiny earthquake of a snowdrop, nothing
To shake the poles too much, just something
To show you've been around and the day holy
Like Sunday or lucky like
The day when a poet is lucky enough to say
Something of importance to himself

That must
Acknowledge and ignore you, the miracle
Taken for granted, being natural,
As the fields turn over, China
Falling as we come up,
And I stand flatfooted on a slanting land
Content with the old lore, with the womb language
That built you with the sun into a rush
Cross to be hung on every door.

COLUMCILLE THE SCRIBE
after the medieval Irish

My hand is weary with writing;
The light quill twitters in my fingers;
Yet here, still, my slender-mouthed pen
Pours a draught for me of dark-blue ink.

My brown hand — O blessed it is indeed
With the stream of God's wisdom pouring from it! —
Squirting the brightness of many inks,
Moves happily till leaf after leaf is lit.

Ah, my little pen, it moves on
Across the plain of books in holy words,
And without ceasing makes, though I am tired,
Cyphers that suddenly take wings like birds.

MAGNA MATER

A dove plus an
Assenting virgin is
An odd equation; the bird of Venus, the
Shotsilk woodhaunter and
A country shawl
In congress to produce
The least erotic of the gods.

Afoot on Sunday, walking green
The little roads or high
In the spring carts, they come to Mass;
Hundreds who know man,
For whom no string was plucked
Or any heavens
Thrown open;

No dichotomy
Affects the prayer; that heaven
Should have one love, and earth another seems
Entirely natural.
What Troubadour
Built this country chapel?

And out of what
Substance? Harping on what nerves?
Mothers here
All virgin, fathers none,
The child a gift of heaven
And held in common by
Each virgin mother.

O indestructible
Country mulch the Muses tread
So delicately, into the earth you go
Breeding, tending
Where flowers are born with the names of kings
You never heard of, pagan fellows
Whose histories and business
Are open secrets in your
Sunshining faces.

MONUMENT X

Stone has gone, no
God clamours nowadays to be
Let out, or even to beat
Inside barbarously in the menhir's heart.
Stonehenge is archaeology.

Unlike that old raw
Obelisk where all streets meet
In the middle of my town, origin
Unknown; Galway masons
Helped it struggle to its feet,

Or I hope so, for
It belongs. Countrymen heel carts
There and pen sheep, boys
Play marbles; sometimes
Old women sit there with baskets

Of fowl, eggs, fish; and politicians
Make speeches after Mass.
Mostly, however, it survives alone,
A weather buttress, dowsing all the rains
Of the green run-down littoral,

But coming out drowsily into
The sun, with the meanings of an old man
Or a shell leftover, something gone
That beat once,
Like a poem in

A lost language like early Erse, this being
The one battered undiscipherable stanza
Surviving. And it's only now
I begin to be curious. My God,
I think, is there something that I missed,

Some saint lying in
The state of God, a mine still working
Gold under us that we have forgotten,
Who never made the pious book
Like those of Syria or Antioch,

Liguria, Carthage, or High Germany,
Like Ursula, Thecla, Donato of Arezzo,
Clement, Susanna, Felicitas,
Blaise of Sebaste, barely glimmering,
And the seven Sleepers of Ephesus,

Innumerable lights
Of what never was on land or sea,
A fugue of heavenly figures
In sarcophagi like this, martyrs blessed
With names that have come down to us.

And I remember
Trooping to the top of the stone just
Such a galaxy. Or do I? My God,
I've sat there in patched shorts,
In the very weather of the thing, and must

Scratch my head to remember if
They were there
Clambering stiffly out of the masonry up
To some miracle above
In the grey Galway air:

134

And I can't even remember now
If our rough masons summitted the job
With a cross that caught the whole East, or
With a blunt piece of Galway stone
Fathered forth some local Priapus.

Which is discouragingly ambiguous
And proves nothing except I'm not the man
I thought I was.
Still, some saints were oddly built,
Like Januarius,

Protector of Naples, Bishop
Of Benevento, who, thrust into fire
By the bloody Pagan walked out whole,
And nobody saw how in the martyr
Two faces clashed beneath the mitre.

Others had older shadows too,
The mast-top twins igniting in the blast
Above the shipping? Enough of that.
Gods live the deaths of one another.
But stone, now, is old hat.

COAT OF ARMS

On Sundays the marvel
Was there early, like
A white stag in the grazing. Up the long
Lane to the belfry we children hung
On the feet of an old Mass-going man;
And it was making;
It was our turn to be looked upon

As if for once we
Had some distinction, the fields unyoked and
Turned loose, all occupation gone
But the business of man
In the holy city
That had no spires
Visible or choirs, a faint angelic land.

Nevertheless we
Stand there in a tree of neighbours,
Our feet in the
Broken artery of a bog village
Till the bell summoned us
To the other side of
The walled world that could be ours.

And I am already afraid
And suffering a mystery
That turns cold the faces the summer sun
Edges gold;
The strong are down upon their knees,
The ogham heads are
Bowed to the happenings on an altar stone.

Heraldic the
Manwoman who
Feeds the fire there, dilating into
Hands that lift, bless, flow:
We belong to a journey into air;
Bell and gong
Announce our presences elsewhere.

Come back.
I sweat it at the side
Of Sunday man, feeling the static shake
In a tide of invocations. Now Monday seems
Most kindly for its implements
And farm animals, all men
At home in the homely house of flesh

Drudging in stone fields
Or high on the creeled cart marketing.
Miracle is
The priest's portion
And the Latin
That came down the muletracks where Hannibal
Stalled with his elephants.

It ends;
Fiat est, and
What was to be accomplished is done;
Deflates with the harmonium;
But not quite, for out there
Hanging in the blue or
Alighted in the unyoked fields is a Sunday air

Mild and
Antlered in trees, that follows
And retreats, that will neighbour us
All day, our playfellow
And almost come to hand;
And begone by tomorrow when
Monday takes over the land.

THE MOTHERS

The Mothers always know it for a lie.
Love me, they say, love me alone;
I am the mystery.
But having separated from her bone
We find the way of our new skeleton
Expanding towards the sky.
For every man is Adam and the tree
His own celestial geometry.

But the birth that divided us is always pain.
The wrench is there for gain or loss;
Two never one again:
For when the tree towers the God is jealous
And our myth always melting about us
Is so much rain,
Till something in the structure starts to give;
Our tall Euclid brings forth Eve.

Here's our second heart. And for all its loveliness
Flesh never learns the techniques of persuasion;
A man is still a nakedness
Under his tree, and cold is the God's gaze on
The white fork where a rose marks the division:
O never again first Oneness.
Divided from it by the Mother's knee,
All poetry is our apology.

To the God the dignity; ours the shilling and the curse
And a heart divided in itself to mourn
Its own divorce;
Half-willing to be still a tower to heaven,
Half-willing to be the dark where love is given
Always for the worse:
A demi-god caught half-way up a cross;
And below, the woman who bemoans his loss.

BOOK OF JOB

The simple thing is to die
So often and so painfully that I
One day in one breath
May live the whole life of death.

The daily thing is to be
Defeated daily, that this psychology
Of victory be unlearned
And sham into shame be turned.

For this Image is not Me;
This worldling satisfied and stately, with his family
Thanksgiving, and each day success,
The world always answering yes.

In this gift of luck I have lost
The naked traffic of the ghost,
Trapped in an image I projected
Not of God but God's elected.

So the next thing is to ride
Horse and all under and be no more a pride;
No, nor an humility,
For that's a pride too, on one knee.

But to be nothing till
Flesh fall off and my heartbeat sounds real;
Until my heart is heard
Stammering with excitement its one word.

Come then rags and plagues,
I am honoured to lend you my legs;
Enter this suffering house
Where honours fall off, where I delouse,

And bless me no more, You
In the twittering evening: O Tall fall of dew,
You fathered me so much ease
I ponder all misery now to find my peace:

I have my occupation; I will die
Into nothing after nothing, but live no lie,
Stripped to a faint shiver, waiting here
On a faint illumination in the air.

V

ODYSSEUS

Last year's decencies
Are the rags and reach-me-downs he'll wear forever,
Knowing one day he'll sober up inside them
Safe in wind and wife and limb,
Respected, of unimpeachable behaviour.

Meanwhile he goes forward
Magniloquently to himself; and, the fit on him,
Pushes his painful hobble to a dance,
Exposing in obscene wounds and dilapidation
The naked metre of the man.

His dog will die at sight of him,
His son want fool-proof, and his lady-wife
Deny his fingerprints; but he
With his talent for rehabilitation
Will be his own man soon, without ecstasy.

ORESTES

Black oracles
That bid the tall son slay the mother
Follow on the heels
Of the lover
Coming to take him over.

Purgation past,
The fiddles play the young bride from behind
Curtain and ghost.
Is the bridegroom blind?
The son out of his mind?

This is vengeance
Outside all sense, beyond all reason
And resonance;
Mother and son
To marry so and be one.

POET PASSING

Never heed this idle fellow. Tool
Your forks, knives and wet spoons around
The pink geranium; shine
Steadily in those meagre constellations and
Dish up for your man:
Keep those bare arms out of the window pane.
The heavens are jealous of the woman
Who suddenly becomes a poem.

Like this it starts, two arms
Tending the beam, the rest of you
Unseen as yet, unborn. Bathsheba showed no more,
And there was adultery.
Watch out now, his nose is in the weather,
Antennae twinkle on the buzzing head,
Now the myths will bounce you off
The moon or some odd marriage bed.

There, he stops his gallop. Doom sealed
You're for it, lady. Tomorrow you'll
Articulate another body, be
Canzone or country ballad. Your own man won't know
Your decent rump.
Goddess, kitchenwoman, whore
Fare no better with this pimp
Who translates all into his mighty hunger;

And even now burgles
Your modest garden, where
Your intimate washing dances on the line.
No lecherous bible king has eyes like his;

But how they gyrate for him, the
Simple cloths, the many
Indefinite nymphs you are
Holding forth upon a bit of twine!

And how he hangs over
The wall, the sea-shelled lime, the native stone.
Under the low apple how the air
Wantons with you, lady. How
Lost he is in wonder.
No man has ever seen you thus, no other
But the openmouthed zephyrs ever
Received you so loud and clear.

Great God, he's at the door now.
A cup of milk? A drink of water? Fly, or
Contain yourself, my dear, in
Your own simple fiction.
The woman suffers metamorphosis
Who heeds this tough.
That's how the story goes.
He finds like the vine a thousand soft dark eyes

That plead for him. He's all
Libation now and ceremony, shy,
Desperate as the young stag horned in the tree.
But mark that eye,
He's on the run, lady. Never
Will he belong to any other
But the virgin breast and great white limb,
The goddess who set the dogs at him.

DELUGE

The winter was without end;
The walk of youth legaway from a bogged-down calendar;
The old left behind
With the blind and the helplessly married
To climb their cocklofts and wait
For the ditchwater fields to push up another level
And the mossgreen belfry toll of itself.

That was a season
In the city and worse; the broken glass of the weather
At every corner;
People passing by with last year's faces;
The very spouts were walking,
Lovers erased, washed from the warehouse doors;
But such copulation the whores wore boots and furs.

The sea so piled, so much
It could not, swore the tidewaiters, possibly be more;
Yet such it was.
That was the time of boredom, of terrible ennuis
Afflicting virgins and true believers;
We had suffered before such innundations
Only when He numbered himself with our enemies.

And then one day
In a lane no wider than your hand a woman
Leaned out of a fug
Of food and napkins and found an air so mild
She hung the goldfinch out,
Loitering while the little bird perked up and sang
To gossip with another window over the way.

LOST MAN

In an old green book, mouldering
From the window ledge, sitting under
A lamp globe made in Bohemia,
I read once how to grow turnips;

In a tiny thatched house where a ladder
Cocked up to a loft above the kitchen,
Simple as the first working skeleton,
Warm as the breastwork of a pigeon;

With a cobbled yard to the little local road
That was kitchen too with a sky roof,
Ruled by an old matriarch who still spun wool
On a wheel of bog oak:

Byres, carthouses, turfricks, pigstyes,
The place was open as a bird's nest
To the weather, the fields, the planetary animals,
The sun had his corner like another beast.

Neighbours too, nodding in, or high
On a creeled cart, mobile in a geography
That never moved till Sunday,
Were names, roots, lineage, graphs and grafts of the one
    tree,

Our gossips, our daily dialogue; in
An odd way too the faces of their fields
Showed through them, the tilt of thatch or turfrick
An aura about them, their identities.

So reading by the bright wick, with
A large moth tapping out the vague
Morse of a summer's night
And the old lady at her steady wheel

Earth rolled small enough to
Be caught in the heartbeat. It was small
As I and manageable, spun to no savage foot;
And my need was to be rooted in the soil

I knew, with a village for a capital,
A spire on Sunday where a local God
Woke up to find some majesty above
The weather or the weekday sod

Where in his working clothes, in grace and grain
And grass he forgot his cherubim and trumpets,
Walked boundaries, was amenable to ewes
And quiet moonbodies like fat turnips.

Mine, of course, was a crop that never grew,
Or could be grown,
Being a life where an old girl used a wheel
Of bog oak, adze-hewn

And sand-honed by a country master long
Before the making of her world
Who laboured by diplight or hearth's glow
Till the thing worked.

FOR PADDY MAC

I

Once, so long ago,
You used to probe me gently for the lost
Country, sensing somehow in my airs
The vivid longlipped peasantry of
Last century

And those bronze men pushed
With their diminishing herds far out on
The last ledge of original earth,
Fomorian types
In the big one-eyed sky

All messed up with sundogs and
Too many rainbows, and that wishwashing head of Bran
In the toppling arches seaward sailing and singing
On his weathered maypole from
A caved-in skull.

Ours were the metres
Of early waters, the first argosy hardly home
With new women, orgies
When the moon rode round
Stone circles counting her twelve.

Homer's people.
And wasn't I lucky, born with
Boundaries floating, language still making
Out of the broadlands where my fathers
Tended their clouds of ewes?

Bunkum, Dear P. The thing was gone, or
Never was. And we were the leftovers,

Lord-ridden and pulpit-thumped for all our wild
Cudgels of Gaelic. Ours was Lever's
One-horse country; the bailiff at the bighouse door.

And hags hung all day
In turfsmoke among the fowl where I was licked.
That was a town
Walled and towered as Troy, and never sieged for a
      woman:
Trading bullocks and pennies for glory gone;

And watched from the top of a shilling the homespun
      fellows
Selling their spades on hiring days,
For a year and a day the dear flesh off their bones
From penury to slavery,
The soul thrown in for a spare.

That was my country, beast, sky and anger:
For music a mad piper in the mud;
No poets I knew of; or they mouthed each other's words;
Such low powered gods
They died, as they were born, in byres.

Oh, maybe some rags and tatters did sing.
But poetry, for all your talk, is never that simple,
Coming out of a stone ditch in the broadlands
Newborn, or from
The fitful pibroch of a lonely thorn,

Or old saws at winter fires.
Muted the big words. Love was left
To eloping earls or such
Lest the snake creep up, usurping the ancient timber
And some odd bloom come bursting from the Cross.

II

And you speak of Raftery, that bold tongue, the tramp
In borrowed bootleather, those rainy eyes
Lifted to empty heaven from a blind man's stick;
I sang like him you say, and praised women,
And I had the true cow's lick;

You who should know how every poet must
Baptize first the font and the very waters,
And have no godfathers but this great thirst
For what is not;
And no mothers;

Who must quote Ambrose crookedly (Nam quid divinius
Isto ut puncto exiguo culpa cadet
Populi), bog Latin for
The bit of earth we tread
Into metaphor

Knowing we're just another civilisation
To be dumped, but go on, say it you,
We've eaten all the Gods yet bow the knee,
And are only really at home
In the larger toleration of the poem.

Carefully, now that you are dead,
I must amend the scribbles of the tribe
Lest sheepman and bullhead
Become a frieze of fathers like stone man,
Hieratic, almost Egyptian,

And from the uncreated, with arms widespread,
From puncto exiguo, beyond the dead
And Lazarus rising, where God is making still
Release the flood
Of living images for good and ill.

Dear P. I'll never know
What you brought over and passed on,
But this seems certain as I grow:
Man lives; Gods die:
It is only the genuflection that survives.

TOTEM

They knew it, the Totem people, the world
Inside the world where man
Makes metaphors
For the animal.

And all this day it intrudes, static
Of older inhabitants, saurian, aborted wing, flipper, fur,
And the wavelengths thereof
Babbling of a broken covenant

Because an old sick cow was put down;
Murder, they say: as if blood shed
From sheer pity dyed
The ghost red,

Set horns tangling in the thicket
And heaven to collapse, as it must
To every act of treachery, in
A jangle of broken trust,

Our mutual world
Impossible with images
Of pain; today
An old lady bled herself away

In Flatfield on the headland; into
October she went, the day lying
To its grass anchors
In autumn scent.

Plumbing her mound soon will be briar and berry;
Deathbed for a Muse,
A post mortem to go on
Forever in the dogrose

Wherein this old shambling skeleton in rawhide
Is totally translated and taken over:
Here in a way lies
Everybody's mother

Confusing certain formal issues, an
Ambiguous body at best, straddling
Source and origin like
The first dolmen,

Requiring the old almost religious
Liaison, from whose
Mysterious totem bones I must ask pardon
For a pact broken

Thus acknowledging the ancient status
Of a quite ordinary creature who yesterday
Was horns not halo, whom heifers
Followed, whom we put down

By the haw hedge, cress and water near
And the orchard
That tells the weather to the falling apple
And rounds the echo travelling towards Tuskar.

FARMER

Last winter a Snowman; and after snow an Iceman
Shattering, O cold, his bright blue limbs like glass
With every frozen footstep; in the thaws that followed on,
A doll that almost melted into mud without a face.

What of it. The sun's in his hands now, hands of iron
That run too with the soft spark of clay,
His look is mild and large as the horizon,
He loses himself in the earth like a summer day.

But how he will come to you, woman, gathering up
His body in a thunder off the grass
In a four-legged gust, he's away and over the fields
     apace —
Tallyho, tallyho — with the whole wild earth at a gallop:
Just beckon, he'll roar up like weather, only to sway
So softly down you'll think him the month of May.

FIELD OBSERVATION

There died last night
In a poor thatch that whiskered heavy man
Who used to go my road
Peaceful as Saturn and as countrified;

In a flit of moonlight,
With the town dwarf complaining in his sleep,
He left corpse and corner,
A broken pot and one bright glass of water.

No more will all things cast
His measure, horoscope or the great size of his breath,
Who was each year reborn
In the annual excursion of the corn;

Who moved in the gravity
Of some big sign, and slowly on the plough
Came out anew in orbit
With birds and seasons circling him by habit;

Morning fell upon
His horses, and the weather moved behind;
From cold Christmas he
Moved up the hill in every leafing tree.

Now the windy fallow
For harmony must invent him in its turn,
Whiskers, seeds and eyes,
His bags about him and his flapping skies;

One day the low-fired sun
In hedges bare and barbed as rolls of wire,
An old stiff half-rayed figure, the sole reason
For each divulging season;

In hayloads lost in June, in
Autumn the wheaten man, while
At their harps together
His strawpale daughter tinkle in the weather;

No other kin, not one
Beam from the blues in the cold cowyards round
The mountain where the crows knew him but never
The women clinging to the winter flaws;

And leaves no name
A season won't erase, old Walrus-face
Who lined the surging team
On a long furrow straight as the morning beam.

MEETING

Countryman, consumptive;
Some children, four, I believe:
Now burned by a sun of another colour,
Tells me again good-morning — sir.
This is truth, too, in one posture.

And easily related
To something already much stated
But always forgotten till a feeling thinks for me
The moment-to-moment philosophy
Of my overpressed mortality.

It does not moralize,
This feeling, but accepts that a man dies
Daily and wearily; the portents are too plain,
Time running out through every vein,
The face the terminus of pain;

Continuously arriving there
Without shock and secretly, but almost bare
And terrified already. I could stand
And talk of seasons and the land,
But he'd see through me and understand.

And hear under my breath
Words that condole with my own death
That seems so distant now, and me too
Sounding the bull-head of my strength, anew:
Spitting where he must swallow down the chew.

SPECIAL FOR NANCY'S MOTHER

Gentle lads, I know
Big moments are
Bodies with heartbeats, outlasting
Sun, moon and star;

That hill-struck with
The sheepmen, high
The weather perches on your looks,
The mountain stares you squarely in the eye;

And is yours, all
The youth and the big views of
Small boys become soul
And love

Where, up here and forever,
Boys you are,
Bodies of place and moments
You scarcely remember

Which are your life now and
Illumination;
Death being merely
Life's big double, the larger twin,

And you still happen,
Wake with morning on
The top pastures, push
The boat into the sun,

Are two brothers with a sister, are
Scree and sky
Between the two waters,
Are all the eye

Ever beheld or the heart felt;
Day never done,
Night still a golden place
With a sleeping sun.

So, dear boys, having all
The footprints, welcome
A new brother, where
Forever you are at home;

And show him
Gravely around yourselves, with
The grand manner of natural powers, like
Weather or myth,

Who stands gravely too
At your threshold, waiting
The almost visible smile,
Your almost visible greeting.

A LOOK IN THE MIRROR

Those iron men!
The Indian wings his way upon an arrow;
Pale blue the sailor
Saunters on the sea;

And the farmer's boy,
Drinking his diesel, eats up the earth,
Spitting out the stones:
These never dwindle down in ink;

Nor Million Dollar
Heavyweights, nor does the Spaceman thrown
Against the dartboard of the moon,
For theirs are necessary capers;

These are the lovely eternal brutes:
All time's bravura, the hailed and the well;
Let us drink to them a foam of ale;
And in the glass consider you

Whom some half-truth stuns
Now autumn ravishes; yet still possessed
By the savage script of the young man,
By the savage dictation,

A heart out of plumb,
And time out of mind, his head
Turned back on his shoulders, nodding
To a drunken line.

A question then,
Why thumb a disconsolate nose
At these marvellous fellows, you with that in-looking face
Your own mirror hardly knows?

THE HOUSE

I stare at it again;
One should remember one's own birth, the first
Fact. The act
Of creation begins there
Where the apple burst.

It's empty air
More or less, the place built over
And a new house settled down
With a shop on the ground floor.
The man born here is a displaced person

And can act only
If up there, an inset in the first storey,
The weightless midwife still
Removes him from the womb, the outrage
Accomplished but unending, never final.

So let candles go
About the four brass knobs, the mother lie
Broad as the seventh day at peace with me;
A flowery wallpaper encloses her
Above the gulps of geography;

Far east, Port Arthur and the yellow threat
Of the little ricemen, battleships gone down;
And the day so mild here and drifting
Soft airs from Clare, the bare trees
Budding rain. History is made at home

Such as it is, and the round world
Established incessantly, like me from you,
On crumbling fronts, instant history
Up to the last pain and the final assault on
The tower of your modesty.

It was late and long
When I came you said, the leaking balloon
Of day deflated in the fields, eight
By the clock or near it, a moon
Occulted in Capricorn, the shuddering sign

That bears Christs and splits the calendars;
Eight by the clock and from my lodging in you
I issued forth
To take up residence in the usual fears,
Loves and longings of the starbacked earth.

Lean back now and still,
Labour just over, the teapot on the hob;
Ignore the signs.
That big black head may be heretical,
But you did your job.

Lean back I say, forever there,
My passport into things;
Name the world for me, who passes by
Name the mudladen streets and who drops in;
And name your son who's starting to begin.

PAINTING OF MY FATHER

I

I saw him to the last, the grey
Casting of the face,
The crabbed hands like this
Yielding to the cluster of the Rosary;

I who barbered you occasionally
And filled your pipe
Dropping into your deafness the odd item
Of family news that never
Exactly reached you,

For you were away already.

So your true going was a sort
Of mutual release. 'Lord', you whispered hanging
That day in my arms naked
As Jesus down from the cross,
'Take me away'.

Now for me this vague distress
And a guilt that grows;
What is it that one owes a father?

And cannot pay,

Liaison lost with the broad
Dialect of the child where words
Were the throbs of a countryside

Big like a sheepshearing or small
As the lark pinned high above
The water meadows where we drank our tea,
The trout waiting in the fishing river;

Eternal precincts
Of a huge present tense, as if
You were not due to be left
Abandoned like an old
Settlement;
The young being
Unscrupulous in their growing up.

So you wanted little of me towards the end,
Barbering, a light
For the old pipe,
And an ear, my ear, any ear, when you spilled over
The intolerable burden
Of being a very old man;

II
An image that wounds;
Better even
The figure of power, the
All father,
Jahwah, Helios or another; not
That I'd like you in big translations
Who were rich enough
As your own man

For you were daylight's own fellow and over
The moonsuck of the mother
All male and master under heaven;

And that's how you come into mind,
In taut middleage when you were quite
The masher,
Velvet collar, tan velour
Overcoat, plush hat and handmade boot,
In those streets round the cattlemarket where
Our evenings were a summer saunter;

Hanlon's Corner, Stoneybatter,
The Broadstone, MGWR,
Where trains run no more,

And I half expect round any corner
The hastening dandy, country
Things still clinging;
Blue the gaze;
Delicate the gait, the dancer,
Angler, Fowler, Hurler, football player;

Tomorrow
Formally as a bullfighter he'll pace
The horned pens and the cattle slobber,
Face the loss or net the profit
Stonily
As befits the gambler;

And at noon lean
Recomposed on the railed wall
By the City Arms, yarning, true Ulyssean,
Over a shoe shine.

III

And now here
Above the walnut desk, the only familiar in
This strange hallucinatory land I found
Late, you stare out; again
All age, all pain, at the very end
Of your long span: not you indeed
But every man;
Just waiting.

Land's End some few miles away; the tide
Is white round the Mount; a bird
Stands on the sundial on the lawn; Spring
Is hovering;
And in the tulip tree — hallucination — some
Medieval person reads a tome

(To disappear battered
By a rainshower with his
Monkshood, creature of air;
The bird stays on, real enough;
A woodpecker)

A country ironed out
Into saints and menhirs where
You never put a foot,

Where the weather camps for an hour before
It stamps the soft shires, taking over
The whole south of England at a blow.

POEM FOR MY MOTHER

I

That dismal country, Killimore-daly:
When my mother talks I know the place at once
And the faces of a century
All dead, but household gossip since;
And again she is my
Dream and my anatomy;
And my geography's that low blue knoll
Over the bog where the black miles are all
To the sky's far wall.

The first on her tongue is that gentle and precise
Grand-uncle James. He tilled the arable
And was a sacrifice
To ties I'd think intolerable.
He was a second son; and one night
When his elder brother's horse took fright,
The cart upturned, and with his brother dead
He found himself with a family ready-made;
And no woman in his bed.

A homely stately man, with an old oaken
Dignity and a courtly way of speech
That left unbroken
The delicate things in a child's reach:
To six girls he was
More than their looking-glass;
And I with my mother's eyes upon me see
The simple and major figure she'd wish on me,
The father I refuse to be.

James was a Dilleen. My mother's mother's people
Were the fair-haired Burkes from the bridge at Raford;

Millers, whose old green wheel
Still grinds for a neighbour's board;
Beech and the bubbling poplar
Ride up the small trout-water
To the sheltered slates where once a harsh-faced wife,
Frank Burke's second woman, spent her life
And her good man's in strife.

A family legend, she; not kind it seems
To step-children. There was some whispered talk,
So my grand-uncle James,
The sturdy man, in his riding cloak
Rode out one winter night
To do the thing was right;
He downfaced the woman on her hearth, he took
The child from the coals and wrapped it in his cloak;
Her lullaby his gentle look.

Pride of that night-ride's in my mother's eyes
When she talks of it. I hear the horse-hooves on
White frost, the stars and trees
Are Christmas; in the lamp six girls listen
And open the door to a call
To take a child like a doll
From an old man's arms — no, not a doll, a rose;
Rose of his heartbeat, as if his life's repose
Had flowered in his frozen clothes.

II

But the woman of the mill, that temper on a hair
And the pride that's an appetite for self-destruction,
She's the one lays bare
The bones of chronicles: no ruction
But the terrible cerebral bitch

Of a self-regarding bitch
Will not stir up, as if she found each place
Dull as a mirror, but in all wild displays
The life inside her face.

The Mill landlord was a jackboot in
The older style, but fair. He called one night
And asked Burke for possession
Of a park he'd leased. He'd all the right,
So Burke agreed. But the door
Opened and his wife with a glare
That silenced him, strode in convulsed and red
And threw a bag of sovereigns at his head:
Fight the bugger, she said.

Take this, the whole strongbox, and till it's spent
On law I'll never have enough of law,
Says she, O the termagant.
And law she had till out-at-elbow,
With Frank dead and the rent
Overdue, she went
Out of the chronicle to America;
Unmourned, unhonoured, even disliked in her day,
But a person in her own way.

She touched her time, but never the people; strange
For her quarrel was the quarrel of the time
When a land-squabble could arrange
Banners and processions and walk out in rhyme:
Does the country, in one who struts,
Guess the illness in the guts
Seeking a tall and suicidal end?
Whom the gods wish to destroy will find no friend
Where all are wise and bend.

III

She was a figure of pride. There was another
Not far away, one of the quality;
And he, says my mother,
Had all the country's sympathy.
His name was Dominic John
Burke-Browne, a gentleman
Of blood so ancient it had lost the sting;
His home was a Norman keep, a naked thing;
The house a plastered wing.

Two sisters, spinsters, this proud bachelor had
With vague accomplishments. In rainy grandeur
One of the two went mad
And wandered the callows with goose and gander:
And when they'd drag her home,
Her neck stretched out in the spume
Of an angry goose, she'd hiss, they say. The other
Had buried her youth without much fuss or bother
And liked that Burke my grandmother:

So much that from the castle the soft fruit came
In baskets down the lane on summer days
From a Burke to a Burke, poor name
That used such different umbrellas;
And, gesture from kin to kin,
A man with a delicate cane
And the carpet walk of the sheltered bookman trod
The winter time up to his heels in mud
That the royal thing confer with its blood.

Old privilege, though he was a Catholic,
Had made it customary he should pray
Curtained away from Mick
And Pat on Sunday and Holyday;

But some Maynoothman with
No reverence for myth
Ruled that all men when down upon the knee
Before the Lord were the one family tree;
And took away his canopy.

He never passed the font again, they say:
And strangely no one blamed him. They had pity
For the proud old man on Sunday
For there in one high window he
Was seen to raise the glass
When bells rang out for Mass
And face the little chapel over the trees,
Missal in hand, upon his bended knees.
And no one felt at ease.

O the stories told about him. There were three
Fools in the parish, three old brothers who
Stole turf nightly;
And wondering if it were true
They were such fools, he set
A trap for them, he put
A crown-piece on a style between the quicks
They'd need to climb to play their usual tricks
On his Nobility's turfricks.

They came at dawn, sluggards, one, two, three
Homespun men, the eldest first as of right;
He passed unseeingly;
But the second saw it — and with no second sight:
Wondering, gibbering, he
Showed it and the three
Filled a pipe and passed it round and round.
To contemplate the better what they'd found,
They sat upon the ground.

A silver piece, and it could have been the moon
That had fallen down for all the complicated
Wonder it brought them. One
By one the younger were animated;
But the eldest, a man of laws,
Pondered all his saws
Till he found that which removed perplexity;
Says he, to each day that day's task, if it be
The turf today, then tomorrow we'll gather money.

The crown was returned to its place, the moon to the air,
And one by one they climbed in their innocence
A style and a townland's laughter.
But O Dominic, man of sense,
Were you the wiser, you
Who gave yourself to the blue
And bookish fiction and denied the red
Blood that clamoured for a girl in bed
And bedamned to the esquired dead?

What had you, O delicate hail-fellow to a book,
More than those slovenly louts who warmed their shins,
You, too, on the hook
Of a logical witless innocence,
You shown the chapel door
By a world you knew no more.
Your dispensation done, who yet strove still
To live your lie, who never lived your will,
Upon your purple hill?

IV

So much for Dominic Burke-Browne. He died
When my mother was young, and some herdsman
    moved in
And never, they say, thrived.
A place to end, not to begin;
An inimical place
To people born on the grass
Whose business is weather and the tillage patch,
All the simple traffic that needs no latch
Between fields and the thatch.

Ghosts, says my mother: And perhaps the dead can throw
Shadows sometimes that the living see.
One is a Dutchman who
Got the castle after Aughrim as his fee;
Not to enjoy it forever;
One night in an embrasure
When he struck a spark to light his pipe the wall
Glowed like a Dutch interior, and some tall
Burke blasted him with a musket ball.

She names ghosts one by one in her chronicle.
One story's funny. Three men sought shelter there;
Two were tall, so the middle
Of the bed was the small man's share;
All night his sleep was lost
For some Euclidean ghost
Whose delight was symmetry tugged till his feet lay
By the tall man's feet, then after some delay
Violently tugged the other way.

V

Tale after tale she tells that brings me back
To a townland that's almost woman to me,

175

To the heart before the crack,
To the peace before the poetry;
Back farther where the earth
Is my pre-natal birth,
Even beyond you, woman, who are tall
As the Mother of God, to your own watery knoll,
So blue where black miles are all.

Between Attymon and Cloonshicahill, between
Lisduff and Brackloon, Woman, O my Maid,
In a townland never seen,
When all townlands were in your head,
You must have imagined a son
And he when your time was done
And it was his turn to seek your face inside
Discovered not a mother nor a bride
But a living countryside.

In all the levels of my eye you are;
And I divine you, I, your diving fork;
O my discovery of water,
You always here where poems work.
No dwindling woman with
A worn face but the myth
That magnifies, hurts, and satisfies till all
My gaze is gathered up upon the tall
Mountain where Muses dwell.

Be there away, but mostly here beside
My blood, in the humdrum of your chair, be you
Most plainly and abide
As if the fire and lamplight too
Found you a resting place;
Mistress of my house, and let this room be kind
From gazing on you when I draw the blind
On the night outside my mind.

TREVAYLOR

First, this
Prayer, that you the people
Gone over, ghosts, bright
Narcissi, lean into my pool now
And be this poem.

Empty are
All mirrors you do not countenance;
The fabulous water is
Fathomed by no horizons
Till you come, till you appear.

I offer you
Only the barest stems. Sunflowers,
Come! Gather your lives
About me here. People
Me in those local airs

Which were yours, which
Are you, which
I breathe. Your flaws over me,
Let them rise and ruffle,
The colours rich

So that I have
Dimensions beyond me, where
You are form and dimension. Tread my
Mirror hugely, people,
That the great thing appear.

MARCH TWENTYSIX

I

All men rage in royal Lear,
Poor old man,
His winter body out of plan,
His flesh antediluvian;

Knowing the perishable year
Is every old man,
And human nature out of date,
Yet clinging to the butcher's meat.

The head that guttered in the air
Is every old man
Nailed to the body, that bare tree,
Lost in the mutter of geography.

The mad white head, distracted stare
Is every old man
And fellow traveller, burnt out
And come into his second sight.

Leaves afterglows, the borrowed wear
Of every other man,
The raiment of an old mad king,
Some tattered daft Platonic thing.
All men rage in old mad Lear.

II

We put James Starkey down today,
A few of us old friends and went our way;
The last, said we;
Gone the galaxy.

March Twentysix, a raindown day;
A blackbird yielding to one single spray;
Delicate the flute
Lifted above the mute.

Poi s'ascose nel foce
Che gli affina — there too without echo,
Sweetly undone,
Is Lesbia's sparrow, the little one.

No sweet mouth but comes to this,
God Attis too for all that Great Goddess
And heavenly stuff:
Much is man and not enough.

POT SHOT

I tell words that talk in trees, this hill
Is my vocabulary, and when I lie down
The sky seizes me so very quietly
I reflect the sunset, the river and I are one.
And then the gun goes off. Am I that, too?
Thunder and blast? And when the hooves of the echoes
Have galloped over the grass and the field aloofly
Returns to itself and silence on its toes
Cranes to hear a rabbit squeal, am I
The wound that I give, the hurt I hurt, the shiver
That talks so tall in trees, that is the sky,
That explodes in death, yet walks like the wide river
So calmly through the evening that I tame
The world around me till it names my name.

THREE HOUSES

I had no gift for it.
It hung out in the welter of the moor;
A black-faced country staring in

All day. Never did the sun
Explode with flowers in the dark vases
Of the windows. The fall was wrong

And there was uplifted the striking north
Before the door.
We lived in the flintlights of a cavern floor.

It was enemy country too, the rafts of the low
Fields foundering. Every day the latch
Lifted to some catastrophe, such as

A foal dead in an outfield, a calf lost
In a mud-suck, a hen laying wild in the rushes,
A bullock strayed, a goose gone with the fox;

The epic, if any, going on too long.
Nil the glory in it, null the profit;
It was too big for me and full of threat.

A place that glugged green in the vast egg
Of the weather, too littered with rains
And with minor stone-age tragedies like getting wet

Feet in the goose paddock watching
An angel, yes, in the air, in the dusk, taking
A rose petal face out of nothing in particular,

Just happening big out of a glitter,
Unaware of me or the black-avised country where
The half-wheel of the day was bogging down.

Certainly it could have been the moon.
And though I prefer to think otherwise
Nothing happened in the way of ecstasy.

And I took indoors my gawky childhood, still
Unmeasured, through mud and the yard midden
That was acting up and coming into the kitchen

With the milkers, with the men, with the weather,
Feeling as ever that the earth is outside matter
Trying to get in, to get into the very centre

Swamp the sunflowers and stone circles
And all that spirals and wings up, to bring
The tiller back on the old compost heap,

Dung value. Petering out
Like this father-figure at the fire
Crumbling into space, who was something once,

Who was the sage here and the reason, who raised
The roof, begot the tree,
Hedged the apple and built the causeway down

For the postman who never comes, who touched
The harsh sex of the earth that never blooms,
And was gentled by this woman who stands in the door
    now,

The mistress of a few iron pots,
With the bogface looking in and the barbarous furrows.
I tell of my angel and the bright thing is lost

In the cud of cows, in the farming day,
Never to bloom again and wash the air
Towards Clonkeen Carle. I sit down by the fire

And build my nightly stockade in the ash
With an old catalogue, Army & Navy Stores,
And polish two pennies bright

While earth and day go under. Buoyed up
In their bundles on the nightwave are the plover,
Blown with the sweet pith of their bones over, the men

Drift off to visit other outposts of
Man in nameless townlands, moon-swollen damps.
The two old people sit it out,

And humped in the very posture of the womb
On a small stool I ride it too,
The dull incessant siege, on the black orb —
The epic, if any, going on too long.

It's feeling now and dangerous
To touch, when I
Was the crown prince of birds early
With the first cock crowing;
And that was a morning,
My head pillowed and abroad
In the true blue;
Meaning I felt the world awake
And I was a county.

Meaning up heartwise the house awoke
To the call of a country;
Turfsmoke curled from below
And day creaked open;
Dangling on my rafter I
Survey my kingdom,
Open fire and hanging kettle,
The doorway wide,
The feathered collie in the morning beam.

Meaning the big unsteady dawn was waiting
And world still making,
Meaning the smoking cows halfmade
Wavered on the dews;
And there was a snail humped on a bridge
And there was the blackbird pecked him up
And there was the mare I was to ride
Butting a silly liquid foal.
The day was starting to report.

Meaning it zigzagged off the arrow
Head of a woodcock, meaning it caught crows
Burgling a turnip field, meaning it sat
On the old crowman in the oats,
His crossbow more askew;
Green hung the crabapples claws;
Rabbits announced me, here
Comes Twolegs and his totem dog;
The thumped morse went on before me.

Meaning it went up into the breath
Of morning, meaning I bowed before
The bowlegged blackthorn in the gap
Where the sunburst met me.
And I was the bogvoice going up,
I was the beginning bees,
I was the dialogue in the curlew's mouth
And simple as a two-holed pipe;
The ripe fern turning south.

Meaning the sun was sailing me, and all
The call of crows on Lynch's knoll was mine;
And lying down I was
The newest butterfly white and green
Drying its wayward compass on a stone,
And the all around and the all to be
Turning over
To catch the three small chimneys on the hill
Treadling the morning smoke.

Meaning the cat loped after the milker
And swallows chuckled
On the byre beams above the cans, meaning
Pigs sang at the stye gate,

And two old men,
Two lovely raggedy old men gossiped
By the upheeled cart, and morning
Was over, done, gone, and never
To be followed after;

Meaning I,
Catching the sun upon a breakfast knife,
No longer beamed;
Housed I was and never homed again,
A dwindled fellow.
Folded the buzzing miles outside the pane
Where the drunken gatepost leaned
And a single foxglove rolled its bells around
A stick tall as an umbrella.

III: KNOCKROE

The river god sat down
In Summer pools. The Satyrs or their male
Correlatives in Gaelic haunted
Bankside and haycock:
It was that season of the year.

Even the sun searched for the female form.
The dayscreen was hers, night flitted
As if from a halfmoon before her;
Her dayshift over,
She lived upon the scandals of the night.

I was the wooded brute then on the road,
Horns in the night bush. Unlimited
The fight, the free-for-all; no
Woman could cover that
Amount of country, so the country did it,

And blocked her out in capitals of trees
On hills and tapped the air
For delicate lights, as I for words. It went
Hard with me
In the old Landleaguer's house,

Dowsing the summer's water, raking hay,
Handling a horse or footing next winter's turf,
Yet it went gay with me who thought
She must be there, be here,
Would come, would come, all things being right,

Who heard the old men talk, the old men say
Something that belonged to her and me,
Land war or cattle stir, some small
Epic with a lift
Was a tall heroic body we could share,

Shining, one to the other, two top
People with a need for deeds. I trained
Tough for something that would never happen,
But happened daily
And ever would happen, being simply me.

Come you now and take the words that make you,
Oblivious twin, all woman, my one peer;
My dark, my darling, full of rage and grace,
Come, Goddess,
Of all your faces show me just one face.

LOST MAN IN ME

I

He can forgive
Enormous sins with ease; Hitler at his ear
With the drums of delirium
Not too hard to bear;

Nor the little men that sell out
Neighbour and passion. Inside his tree
Equating leaf and trunk
The big is no more than the moiety,

And the hugest trulls beam
The shy lamps of virgins; on the Petrine rock
The worst popes shine like artifacts;
Not theirs the shepherd's crook

But his for who knows
Who corrupted who? Not he who stares
At Messalina in the Roman whorehouse
And wholly admires the wares;

And is not too put out when Catherine
Garrots her man. Behind his fan
He listens to Lesbos singing and the voice
Sweet as duet and duel says all that love can:

Which is neither more or less
Than you, me, sun and moon. He quotes the Hai Ta'u—
'The supreme virtue of heaven is to produce';
And leaves it to me and you,

As if our generals were mere gun
Barrels to a moment that waits upon the trigger.
If any unpin the bomb,
It's in the Thing itself and will it matter?

A round of Yin, then
A round of Yang, that equals the Tao. In
His tree already he forgives them, if
Forgiveness is possible without sin,

As if all
Were turning sweetly on the potter's wheel, the gross
Fungus and the girl about to fall.
The virtue of heaven is simply to produce

Anything. It's a music. Birdsong or bomb,
It's all equal. In his Yin-Yang tree
He doesn't ape God but is quite like some
Kind of eternity

In whose paradox I can sing,
Who sits in my tree
A million-million years doing nothing
But forgiving me.

II
Down there, mast high,
He hangs above the world's waters;
Inch after inch he clambers into the sky
On a wincing rope.
This might be the day to die.

One hand holds, one desperate claw
Battered sea-black, green and blue.
The other tears at the canvas gale;
Lurching on a seatop he
Empties the belly of a sail.

Seabooted, unwieldy, wearing no
Wings he should be foundering down
Latitudes that turn to snow;
Instead, he spins
The rough earth on the axis of one toe.

And with a single ropeyarn he
Tugs east the hugely blackening west.
The compass in his head is true;
All points at rest.
His bird is married to the sea.

This could be the day. He rolls
Surgewise, seeking it. The shiver
Of water piles up to the Pole.
He jumps the nearest backstay down,
Spits in a fist, sails on forever.